Sanctions Architects

Sanctions Architects

The Strategists Who Weaponized Finance

Selma Aarvik

Mindful Pages

Published in 2026

ISBN: 9789376558230 (PB)
ISBN: 9789376555826 (eBook)

Published by

Mindful Pages
Imprint of Alpha Editions LLC
312 W. 2nd St #1834
Casper, WY 82601, USA

This book was developed using advanced writing tools to support the drafting and ideation process. All content has been thoughtfully curated, refined, and reviewed to ensure quality and relevance.

Content

Introduction

In March 2012, inside a low concrete building on the outskirts of Brussels, the servers kept humming. It was a weekday afternoon at SWIFT, the Society for Worldwide Interbank Financial Telecommunication, and the sound in the operations room was the usual one: fans, air-conditioning, the dry clatter of keyboards. Then a sequence of banks was disconnected. Iranian financial institutions, named in a European Union regulation agreed days earlier, were cut from the messaging system that carries payment instructions across borders. No ships were stopped in ports. No diplomats raised their voices. But within hours, oil payments failed to settle. The screen stayed stubbornly frozen. For clerks in Tehran and traders in Singapore alike, the absence of a confirmation message was louder than any speech.

That disconnection is often remembered as a geopolitical turning point, an assertion of resolve by governments determined to halt Iran's nuclear programme. Less remembered are the hands that made it operational. The names on the press releases belonged to ministers and commissioners; the work fell to policy lawyers translating intent into legal text, technocrats drafting protocols, engineers flipping access permissions. They did so under time pressure, in inboxes dense with redlined drafts, with the faint smell of burnt coffee lingering through the night. Those decisions did not feel theatrical. They felt procedural.

The paradox sits in plain view. Sanctions are framed as acts of statecraft, yet their force is applied through ordinary professional routines. They rely on people whose job titles suggest caution rather than coercion: compliance officers, licensing caseworkers, risk analysts. The modern sanctions regime does not announce itself with banners. It arrives as an automated alert, a rejected payment, a relationship quietly terminated. Its most decisive moments occur far from podiums, at desks where the only audience is a blinking cursor.

The idea that economic pressure could substitute for military force is not new. What has changed is where that pressure is applied. For much of the twentieth century, sanctions meant embargoes on goods and restrictions on trade routes. Ships were tracked; cargoes seized. By the early 2000s, policymakers had learned that money moved faster than metal and that control over payment systems could choke activity more efficiently than blockades. In 2001, after the attacks on New York and Washington, the United States Treasury began to invest heavily in financial intelligence, mapping correspondent banking networks and exploiting the fact that dollar transactions clear through a small number of nodes. By the time the Iran campaign gathered pace a decade later, the centre of gravity had shifted decisively from ports to payments.

This shift created a new kind of power and a new kind of vulnerability. When access to the global financial system becomes conditional, the leverage is immense. A bank excluded from clearing cannot easily compensate; alternative channels are costly and fragile. At the same time, the effects propagate in ways that are hard to predict. Payments are systems, not pipes. They depend on trust, timing, and shared standards. Change a rule in one place and behaviour adjusts elsewhere, often in ways that designers did not intend.

Consider the journey of a single designation. In July 2014, after Russia's annexation of Crimea, the European Council agreed to restrict access to capital markets for certain Russian banks. The decision was political, but its execution unfolded through layers. Legal drafters in Brussels specified maturity thresholds and instrument types. National authorities issued guidance. Banks updated screening lists and rewrote internal policies. A relationship manager in Vienna called a long-standing client to explain that a credit line would not be renewed. The concept has a name—implementation chains—but the lived reality is a sequence of judgments, each bounded by incomplete information and institutional fear.

Seeing sanctions as chains is still too simple. They behave more like systems with feedback loops. A restriction imposed to deter a government can, through over-compliance, isolate humanitarian actors; the resulting reports prompt calls for exemptions; exemptions, if poorly designed, fail to restore flows; banks retreat further. In 2018, after the re-imposition of United States sanctions on Iran following Washington's withdrawal from the nuclear agreement, European officials announced mechanisms to facilitate legitimate trade. One such vehicle, INSTEX, was unveiled in January 2019 in Paris. It existed largely on paper. Banks, wary of secondary sanctions, declined to engage. The system registered activity without moving money. The limitation was real and instructive: architecture without adoption exerts little force.

The people navigating these dynamics rarely set out to become instruments of pressure. Many entered their fields drawn by technical puzzles or the promise of stability. A commercial lawyer learns to draft clauses that allocate risk; a data specialist tunes algorithms to reduce false positives; a civil servant assesses licence applications against criteria. Over time, they realise that these micro-decisions shape supply chains and livelihoods. A clause excluding a sanctioned counterparty pushes a supplier to reroute through a third country. An algorithm tightened after a public enforcement action delays a hospital's payment for oxygen concentrators. The abstract becomes intimate.

One of the book's recurring figures is the sanctions architect: not a grand strategist but a professional who designs, maintains, or questions the machinery of restriction. The term is descriptive rather than heroic. Architects work within constraints; they balance load-bearing requirements against human use. In the sanctions context, those requirements include legal defensibility, political intent, and institutional risk tolerance. The human use is messier. It encompasses families waiting for remittances, companies paying wages, aid agencies trying to keep generators running. The architect's drawings are not blueprints but policies, protocols, and code.

The rise of financial sanctions also altered the role of private institutions. Banks became gatekeepers, expected to enforce public rules at private cost. This expectation was formalised through penalties. In 2014, BNP Paribas agreed to pay nearly $9 billion to United States authorities for sanctions violations related to Sudan, Iran, and Cuba. The figure, announced in July in New York, reverberated through compliance departments worldwide. Training budgets expanded. Thresholds tightened. Relationships deemed marginal were severed. The behaviour has a name—de-risking—but its mechanics are behavioural. Fear sharpens caution.

And yet, fear is an imprecise instrument. When institutions over-comply, they create de facto sanctions that go beyond official policy. Entire categories of customers are excluded because the cost of distinguishing lawful from unlawful is deemed too high. In 2017, charities working in Somalia reported widespread difficulty transferring funds, despite humanitarian exemptions, as banks withdrew services to the region. The implication was stark: a tool designed to pressure armed groups was constraining aid to civilians. The system's feedback was slow and muffled.

There are counter-examples, and they matter. Targeted financial measures have, in some cases, altered behaviour without broad harm. The freezing of assets linked to specific individuals involved in corruption in West Africa in the mid-2010s, coordinated through multilateral fora, demonstrated that precision is possible when intelligence is strong and objectives narrow. These successes tend to be quieter, less visible than sweeping campaigns, and they complicate simple narratives of failure. Still, they do not negate the structural tensions inherent in weaponised finance.

Export controls illustrate a parallel evolution. Once anchored in lists of controlled goods, they have expanded into strategies aimed at slowing technological advancement. In October 2022, the United States Department of Commerce announced controls on advanced semiconductor manufacturing equipment destined for China. The rules were complex, tying performance thresholds to licensing requirements. Engineers and lawyers laboured over definitions of "advanced". Case officers evaluated shipments that sat at the boundary between civilian and military use. Factories paused investment decisions. The concept is control logic; its implication is that design choices reverberate across industries.

Evasion follows pressure. As controls tighten, actors search for routes around them. Shell companies proliferate; trade is re-routed through third countries; digital assets are tested as alternatives. Enforcement teams adapt in turn, developing heuristics and sharing typologies. The dynamic resembles a long game rather than a decisive blow. A veteran investigator once described keeping a notebook of familiar tricks: recycled directors, mirrored addresses, sudden spikes in obscure exports. It was not nostalgia. It was pattern recognition.

Humanitarian exceptions sit uneasily within this contest. They are essential to mitigate harm, yet difficult to operationalise. Drafted under political pressure, their wording can be decisive. A licence that permits "food and medicine" may fail to cover fuel needed to transport either. Negotiating with banks to honour such licences requires trust and patience. The work is relational. It involves repeated meetings with risk committees, the presentation of audit trails, assurances that penalties will not follow. When it succeeds, trucks move. When it fails, they idle.

Inside compliance teams, the work is relentless. Alerts arrive by the thousands. Audits loom. Relationship managers plead. The emotional burden accumulates quietly. Decisions that appear binary on a screen—release or block—carry human weight. A diary entry reconstructed from anonymised accounts captures the strain: approving a tuition payment feels like relief; rejecting a medical invoice feels like a verdict. Institutions rarely provide language for this burden. Individuals improvise coping mechanisms or leave.

Secondary sanctions extend these dynamics globally. By threatening penalties on third-country actors, one jurisdiction exports its rules. A banker in Southeast Asia recalibrates client portfolios to maintain access to dollar clearing. A multinational corporation redraws its investment map. Allies negotiate carve-outs to protect their firms, even as they endorse the underlying objectives. The ripple effects reach places never mentioned in policy statements.

Measuring outcomes remains fraught. Analysts attempt to link economic indicators to political concessions, but causality is elusive. Sanctions coincide with diplomacy, internal dynamics, and exogenous shocks. Still, the demand for assessment persists. Researchers compile datasets, compare regimes, argue over metrics. Some campaigns are quietly acknowledged as failures; others are declared successes on contested grounds. Learning is uneven. Institutional defensiveness can be as powerful as analytical rigour.

Within this landscape, doubt emerges. Professionals who once took the system's premises for granted begin to question its justice or efficacy. Some annotate margins. Some speak up. Some leave. Others stay and push for reform from within, advocating narrower designations or clearer guidance. Moral injury—a term borrowed from other fields—captures the dissonance between one's role and one's values. It is not universal, but it is present enough to shape careers.

The motif that runs through these stories is interruption. A payment interrupted. A career interrupted by doubt. A feedback loop interrupted by fear. Interruption is both the mechanism and the cost of sanctions. It is what gives them force and what spreads their effects beyond intended targets. Recognising this does not resolve the dilemmas. It sharpens them.

Still, there is movement. Experiments with mixed strategies, combining pressure with incentives, suggest alternatives to blunt force. Informal networks of practitioners share design principles that prioritise clarity and proportionality. Efforts to bring affected communities into policy discussions challenge assumptions about distance and abstraction. None of this abolishes sanctions. It reshapes them.

The question that hangs over the pages that follow is diagnostic rather than moralistic. Given that finance has been weaponised, how should those who design and operate these tools understand their responsibilities? What trade-offs are acceptable, and who decides? The answers will not be uniform. They will be contested, provisional, and shaped by context. But they will be made, whether explicitly or by default, in offices where the servers hum and the coffee goes cold.

Chapter 1
Turning Payments Into Pressure

On a grey morning in September 2005, a young official at the United States Treasury sat staring at a diagram of bank accounts rather than a map of shipping lanes. The case concerned Banco Delta Asia, a small lender in Macau accused of handling funds linked to North Korea. There were no cargo manifests to seize, no tankers to divert. Instead, the proposal was to label the bank a "primary money laundering concern" and watch what happened next. Within weeks, correspondent banks severed ties. Depositors ran. Pyongyang's access to hard currency constricted sharply. A pressure point had been found not at sea, but deep inside the circulatory system of finance. The move looked technical, even obscure. Its effects were anything but.

For much of modern history, sanctions were imagined as blunt instruments. They were lists of goods and lists of names, backed by the threat of interception. The imagery was maritime: blockades, patrols, seizures. What changed in the early twenty-first century was not merely the ambition of policymakers, but their understanding of where leverage truly lay. Money had become the lifeblood of global trade, and banking its nervous system. Interrupt the signals, and the body faltered. This shift did not announce itself with fanfare. It emerged through memos, pilots, and a growing confidence that financial choke points could do what embargoes often could not.

The architect behind such thinking rarely appears in public histories. One early advocate was a mid-ranking Treasury lawyer who argued, in internal meetings, that targeting correspondent accounts would achieve more than chasing ships flagged under obscure registries. Her reasoning was pragmatic. Ports were plural; payment systems were concentrated. If a bank lost access to dollar clearing, the consequences were immediate and difficult to evade. The idea travelled upward, framed in cautious language, supported by charts rather than rhetoric. When it was adopted, the leverage multiplied. So did the complexity.

Moving pressure from ports to payments altered the texture of sanctions. A ship detained is a visible event; a payment rejected is a silent one. It leaves no photograph, only an error message. That silence proved powerful. It also proved contagious. Banks watching a peer punished adjusted their behaviour pre-emptively. Risk committees rewrote appetites. Relationships once deemed manageable were reclassified as intolerable. The unintended consequences were not accidents; they were emergent properties of a system responding to fear.

Understanding that system requires tracing how an abstract political goal becomes a blocked transaction. The chain begins in rooms where objectives are framed broadly: deter proliferation, signal resolve, change behaviour. Those aims are translated into legal instruments, dense with definitions and thresholds. Regulators issue guidance, often clarifying some ambiguities while introducing others. Banks interpret those signals through internal policies, shaped by their own histories and exposures. Finally, software executes rules at speed, flagging names and patterns. At each step, human judgment intervenes.

A designation agreed by ministers in London in July 2018 might reach a compliance analyst in Frankfurt as an alert hours later. The analyst sees a name match at 92 per cent confidence. The policy requires escalation above 90. The clock starts. Should the payment be stopped pending review? The counterparty claims urgency. The guidance is ambiguous. The analyst decides. This is not theatre. It is labour. And it is here, in these moments, that sanctions acquire their real force.

The distance between cabinet rooms and compliance desks has encouraged a persistent misunderstanding: that sanctions are discrete events rather than ongoing processes. A list is published; a decision is made; the story ends. In practice, sanctions behave more like systems that adapt over time. They generate feedback—economic data, humanitarian reports, evasion patterns—that can inform adjustment or entrenchment. Whether that feedback is heeded depends on institutional design.

One policy aide, working quietly in a European foreign ministry, became convinced that the absence of structured feedback was undermining effectiveness. After visiting aid organisations struggling to move funds under a sanctions regime, she proposed a review mechanism linking humanitarian indicators to periodic reassessment. The idea was modest: not to dilute pressure, but to calibrate it. The mechanism survived scepticism and was piloted. Where it functioned, licences were refined and guidance clarified. Where it was ignored, harm accumulated without strategic gain. The lesson was uncomfortable. Ignoring system effects does not make them disappear; it merely blinds the designer.

Systems thinking sits uneasily with the political appetite for decisiveness. Announcements prefer clarity. Systems prefer iteration. The tension between the two is a defining feature of modern sanctions. It explains why measures can be both under-performing and excessively harmful at the same time. Pressure leaks where it should concentrate; pain concentrates where it should not. Recognising this does not require abandoning sanctions. It requires seeing them for what they are: socio-technical arrangements that demand stewardship.

Out of this recognition emerged a new professional identity. The sanctions architect is not a title conferred, but a role assumed. It belongs to those who design the rules, build the tools, and live with the consequences. A commercial lawyer drafting force majeure clauses discovers that her language determines whether suppliers can exit contracts with sanctioned entities. A risk officer deciding to exit a correspondent relationship realises that entire regions may lose access to remittances. These are not abstract responsibilities. They are exercised daily, often without acknowledgement.

The birth of this identity was gradual. As financial measures eclipsed trade bans, the locus of decision-making shifted inward, into institutions that had not previously seen themselves as instruments of foreign policy. Banks hired specialists; governments recruited from industry. A shared vocabulary developed, mixing legal precision with operational pragmatism. Over time, some practitioners began to reflect on the scope of their influence. They noticed that their decisions were reshaping supply chains, not merely complying with rules.

This chapter follows that evolution. It begins with the moment when finance overtook freight as the preferred lever of pressure, and examines the reasoning that made correspondent accounts more attractive targets than hulls and harbours. It then unpacks the decision chain that carries intent into action, revealing how many hands shape the outcome before a transaction is stopped. Along the way, it treats sanctions not as static measures but as living systems, responsive to incentives and blind to some of their own effects. Finally, it introduces the figure who recurs throughout the book: the sanctions architect, whose ordinary career choices carry extraordinary weight.

The relevance of this shift is not confined to any single conflict or country. Financial infrastructure has only grown more central since that grey morning in Macau. Digital payments accelerate flows; data analytics sharpen detection; enforcement penalties reinforce caution. At the same time, the moral and practical questions have intensified. Who bears responsibility when a lawful payment fails? How much collateral damage is tolerable in pursuit of strategic aims? These questions are not theoretical. They are faced by individuals deciding what is possible, legal, and acceptable under pressure.

A motif threads through the chapter: the narrowing aperture. As sanctions move inward, from borders to balance sheets, the aperture through which money passes narrows. Pressure increases. So does the risk of obstruction where movement is legitimate. The narrowing is deliberate, but its effects are diffuse. Recognising where and how that aperture is adjusted is the first step towards understanding the power that modern sanctions wield.

The story does not offer easy answers. It offers something more demanding: a clearer view of the machinery and the people who keep it running. By the end, the reader is invited to see payments not as neutral conduits, but as contested spaces where policy, profit, and ethics intersect. The pages that follow do not ask for admiration or condemnation. They ask for attention.

From diplomatic tool to financial weapon

On 15 September 2005, the United States Treasury named Banco Delta Asia, a small bank in Macau, a "primary money laundering concern". The designation itself ran to a few pages of Federal Register text, dry and procedural. Yet within days, the bank was effectively cut off from the global financial system. Correspondent banks withdrew. Depositors queued. North Korean accounts held there became unusable. No embargo had been declared, no ship intercepted in the South China Sea. The pressure travelled instead through ledgers and clearing accounts, tightening with remarkable speed. A single administrative act had turned finance into force.

The moment crystallised a shift that had been building quietly for years. Sanctions had long belonged to the diplomatic toolkit, a way of signalling displeasure or resolve when words proved insufficient. What changed in the early twenty-first century was not the existence of sanctions, but their centre of gravity. Trade lists and cargo controls gave way to banking measures; ports yielded to payment systems. The instrument remained political. The mechanism became financial.

The paradox is stark. Trade embargoes are visible, even theatrical. Financial sanctions are largely invisible, yet often more disruptive. One stops goods at the border. The other closes the valve upstream. Pressure concentrates.

The thesis of this transformation is simple but unsettling. By moving the pressure point from physical trade to financial infrastructure, policymakers discovered leverage that was faster, broader, and harder to escape. They also unleashed effects that were more diffuse, more private, and more difficult to reverse. Banking measures did not merely supplement classic embargoes; they redefined what sanctions were and who truly wielded them.

For much of the twentieth century, sanctions logic followed the materiality of trade. If a state misbehaved, access to commodities, technology, or markets would be restricted. The enforcement challenge lay in tracking goods and policing borders. During the

Cold War, the Coordinating Committee for Multilateral Export Controls laboured over lists of strategic items, from machine tools to microelectronics. The assumption was that constraining physical inputs would constrain state capacity. Finance was ancillary, a means of settlement rather than a target.

Globalisation altered that calculus. By the late 1990s, supply chains had lengthened, ownership structures had blurred, and capital moved with unprecedented ease. A shipment could be rerouted; a flag could be changed. Payments, by contrast, remained concentrated. Dollar transactions cleared through a limited number of institutions. Messaging flowed through shared utilities. These were not national chokepoints but functional ones, embedded in private infrastructure yet subject to public jurisdiction. Someone noticed.

That someone was not a single visionary but a cohort of officials and advisers who began to look at banking plumbing rather than trade flows. One of them, a Treasury lawyer working on counter-proliferation in the early 2000s, argued repeatedly that correspondent accounts were the weak joints of the system. Her point was operational rather than ideological. Ships can find new ports. Banks without correspondents cannot settle. The argument gained traction after the attacks of September 2001, when financial intelligence suddenly carried strategic urgency. Mapping money became as important as tracking materiel.

The Banco Delta Asia case provided proof. It demonstrated that a targeted financial action could trigger a cascade of private responses without the need for broad prohibitions. The United States did not ban all dealings with Macau. It did not sanction every bank in the region. It signalled that association with one institution carried intolerable risk. The market enforced the rest. This pattern would recur.

Observe the mechanics. A regulatory designation is issued. Name: reputational contagion. Explain: banks, facing asymmetric penalties and limited upside, retreat en masse. Consequence: isolation exceeds the formal scope of the rule. The effect is powerful precisely because it is indirect.

By the time the European Union and the United States escalated sanctions against Iran in the early 2010s, this logic had been internalised. In March 2012, when Iranian banks were disconnected from SWIFT in Belgium, the decision was framed as technical compliance with EU law. Its impact was systemic. Oil revenues stalled. Letters of credit failed. The country's trade contracted sharply. According to the International Monetary Fund, Iran's GDP fell by more than 6 per cent in 2012. The pressure was real. So was the collateral damage.

What made these measures attractive to policymakers was not only their efficacy but their deniability. Financial sanctions could be presented as regulatory actions rather than acts of economic warfare. They leveraged existing compliance obligations. They were implemented by private actors who bore the operational burden. This diffusion of responsibility suited governments wary of overt confrontation. It also obscured where discretion truly lay.

Classic embargoes had clear lines of authority. A navy enforced a blockade; customs officials seized goods. Banking measures dispersed authority across institutions whose primary mandate was not foreign policy. Compliance teams interpreted rules. Risk committees set thresholds. Software engineers encoded logic. Each layer added friction and judgement. The sanction was no longer a single act but a sequence of decisions.

This dispersion altered incentives. Faced with the possibility of multi-billion-dollar penalties, banks prioritised risk avoidance over policy nuance. After BNP Paribas agreed in July 2014 to pay nearly $9 billion for sanctions violations, compliance budgets swelled and appetites shrank. Entire categories of business were deemed unviable. This behaviour had a name—over-compliance—but it was driven less by ignorance than by rational calculation. The expected cost of error dwarfed the profit of precision.

Here, the motif of the valve matters. Financial sanctions work by narrowing the passage through which money flows. Unlike a gate, a valve can be tightened incrementally. Each institution adjusts it slightly, often without coordination. The cumulative effect can be strangulation. Pressure intensifies not because the law demands it, but because the system responds predictably to fear.

The rise of banking measures also transformed the temporal dimension of sanctions. Trade controls often take months to bite, as contracts unwind and inventories deplete. Financial measures act almost immediately. A payment rejected today can halt production tomorrow. This speed is seductive. It creates the impression of control. It also leaves little time for calibration.

The unintended consequences follow from this compression. Humanitarian actors struggle to move funds even when exemptions exist. Small businesses lose access to finance because their geography resembles risk. Remittance corridors collapse. In Somalia, aid organisations reported severe banking difficulties after 2011, despite explicit carve-outs. The pressure designed for armed groups seeped into civilian life. The valve did not discriminate.

There are limits to this model, and acknowledging them sharpens rather than weakens the argument. Financial sanctions depend on network centrality. Where alternatives exist, leverage erodes. Russia's efforts after 2014 to build domestic payment systems and reduce dollar exposure illustrate this dynamic. While not eliminating vulnerability, such measures complicate enforcement. Similarly, states with limited integration into global finance are less susceptible to banking pressure than trade-dependent ones. Ports still matter.

Moreover, financial sanctions can undermine trust in the system they exploit. Each use invites adaptation. Alternative messaging systems are explored. Bilateral settlement arrangements proliferate. The very efficiency that makes financial measures attractive also makes them visible targets for circumvention. The valve, once tightened too often, may be bypassed.

These limitations do not negate the shift. They contextualise it. Policymakers did not abandon embargoes; they layered them with financial controls. The novelty lay in the reordering of priorities. Banking measures moved from supporting role to lead instrument. With that move came a redistribution of power.

The sanctions architect emerges here, not as a mastermind, but as a professional navigating this reordered landscape. The Treasury lawyer arguing for correspondent targeting was not seeking to weaponise finance for its own sake. She was solving a problem as she understood it. Yet her solution redefined the field. By privileging payment systems over ports, she helped create a regime where leverage is exerted through infrastructure that few citizens ever see.

This infrastructural turn raises enduring questions. Who governs systems that are nominally private but strategically indispensable? How should discretion be exercised when the effects of caution are borne by distant others? What obligations accompany the ability to interrupt livelihoods with a keystroke? These questions did not arise with trade embargoes in the same way. They are products of the financial turn.

The valve appears again in policy debates about calibration. Advocates of "smart sanctions" argue for precision: tighter targeting, clearer exemptions, better guidance. Critics warn that any narrowing risks disproportionate harm. Both are right, in part. Precision reduces some harms while amplifying others. The valve can be adjusted, but never made neutral.

The sharpened choice that remains is not between sanctions and their absence, but between modes of pressure. Moving from ships to systems delivered unprecedented leverage. It also demanded new forms of responsibility. The test is whether those who design and operate financial sanctions can recognise when tightening the valve achieves strategic effect and when it merely transfers pain. The answer lies not in slogans, but in how the system is built, monitored, and questioned by the people inside it.

Mapping the sanctions decision chain

On 6 April 2018, the United States Treasury added Oleg Deripaska and several companies linked to him to its Specially Designated Nationals list. The announcement was made in Washington, D.C., carried instantly by wire services, and framed as a decisive response to malign activity. Within minutes, trading desks in London froze exposures. Within hours, compliance systems in Frankfurt and Singapore began rejecting payments bearing newly toxic names. By the following week, aluminium markets had convulsed, prompting emergency licences and partial reversals. What appeared, from the outside, as a single act was in fact a relay. Many hands touched the baton.

The popular image of sanctions suggests a straight line from political will to economic effect. A government decides. A target suffers. The truth is less linear and far more human. Between the moment a minister agrees an objective and the instant a transaction is blocked lies a chain of interpretation, translation, and discretion. Each link is shaped by institutional incentives, professional norms, and imperfect information. The chain is not a conduit. It is a series of judgments.

The thesis is straightforward. Sanctions do not operate as commands transmitted intact from the centre. They function as decision chains in which meaning is progressively re-authored. Understanding their real effects requires following that chain, step by step, and recognising how authority disperses as it travels.

The chain begins where policy is made, often under conditions of urgency and ambiguity. Political goals are framed broadly—signal resolve, deter escalation, punish wrongdoing. These goals are necessarily elastic. They are shaped by coalition politics, media cycles, and diplomatic bargaining. Observe a cabinet meeting convened after a crisis. The language is moral and strategic rather than operational. Name the problem. Agree to act. Leave details for later. The consequence is intentional vagueness, which allows agreement but defers precision.

That vagueness is handed to legal drafters. Here the tone shifts. Concepts must be rendered into enforceable text. Jurisdiction matters. Definitions proliferate. A term like "control" acquires percentages and tests. Exemptions are carved out, sometimes narrowly, sometimes generously, depending on negotiating power. In July 2014, when the European Union adopted sectoral sanctions in response to Russia's actions in Ukraine, lawyers laboured over maturity thresholds for debt instruments. Was it thirty days? Ninety?

The choice mattered. Banks priced risk accordingly. A political compromise became a numerical rule.

This translation introduces the first major transformation. Observe the move from intention to instrument. Name it legal encoding. Explain that law demands specificity where politics tolerates ambiguity. The consequence is that sanctions acquire edges—bright lines that invite both compliance and gaming.

Once promulgated, legal texts do not implement themselves. Regulators and ministries issue guidance, clarifications, and frequently asked questions. These documents are often overlooked, yet they are crucial. They interpret intent and signal enforcement priorities. After the April 2018 designations, the Office of Foreign Assets Control issued General Licences 12 and 13, allowing limited wind-down of transactions with certain Russian companies. The licences were time-bound and conditional. Market actors parsed every clause. Some interpreted generosity; others saw traps. Behaviour adjusted.

At this stage, the chain intersects with private governance. Banks receive the rules and must decide how to operationalise them. They convene committees, update policies, and reconfigure systems. Risk appetite statements are revised. Training sessions are scheduled. The decisions are collective but not uniform. A global bank with extensive United States exposure reads guidance differently from a regional lender with limited touchpoints. Observe divergence. Name it institutional interpretation. Explain that exposure shapes caution. The consequence is uneven application.

The next handoff is technical. Sanctions lists are ingested into screening software. Name-matching thresholds are set. Algorithms are tuned. A 90 per cent match triggers escalation; an 80 per cent match may not. These numbers are not mandated by law. They are chosen. A data team adjusts parameters after a public enforcement action. False positives rise. So do delays. A hospital payment waits. The decision was not political, yet it was consequential.

Here the motif of the relay becomes visible. Each participant believes they are passing on the baton faithfully. Each adjusts grip. By the time it reaches the finish, it has changed.

The Deripaska case illustrates how quickly the chain can strain. When aluminium producer Rusal was designated alongside its principal shareholder, the legal text did not explicitly ban trading in aluminium. Markets nonetheless reacted violently. Prices spiked. European manufacturers lobbied their governments. Within weeks, Treasury announced a framework to delist Rusal contingent on governance changes. The political goal—pressure on an individual—had collided with systemic exposure. The chain fed back on itself.

Contrast this with a quieter example. In February 2016, following the implementation of the Joint Comprehensive Plan of Action with Iran, many nuclear-related sanctions were lifted. Legal texts were amended. Guidance was issued. Yet banks remained wary. Years of enforcement had conditioned behaviour. Correspondent relationships were not restored. Trade recovered slowly. The chain exhibited inertia. Political relief did not translate into operational normality. Observe lag. Name it compliance memory. Explain that institutions remember penalties longer than promises. The consequence is under-performance.

These examples reveal a pattern. The further a sanction travels from its political source, the more it is shaped by actors whose primary incentives are not geopolitical. Compliance officers are evaluated on avoiding breaches, not achieving foreign policy outcomes. Software engineers optimise for accuracy and efficiency, not proportionality. Relationship managers fear reputational damage. Each acts rationally within their frame. Collectively, they can distort intent.

A credible limitation must be acknowledged. Some sanctions are designed precisely to delegate enforcement to markets. The reputational contagion that followed the Banco Delta Asia designation in 2005 was not an accident. It was the mechanism. In such cases, dispersion is a feature, not a flaw. The chain amplifies pressure by encouraging private withdrawal. Recognising this does not negate the argument; it refines it. The question becomes where delegation ends and abdication begins.

The chain also varies across jurisdictions. In the United States, enforcement is centralised and penalties are severe. In the European Union, implementation is fragmented across member states. National authorities interpret and enforce regulations with varying intensity. A designation agreed in Brussels may be pursued aggressively in Paris and cautiously in Athens. Banks adjust accordingly. The relay crosses borders. Friction accumulates.

Metrics can make this visible. Studies by the Peterson Institute for International Economics have shown wide variation in compliance behaviour across sectors and regions, even under uniform rules. Delays in humanitarian transactions correlate with jurisdictions where enforcement guidance is sparse. These are not moral failures. They are systemic outcomes.

The human judgments embedded in the chain are often invisible to those at either end. Ministers rarely see the alerts their decisions generate. Customers rarely understand the provenance of a rejection. The opacity breeds mistrust. Targets accuse banks of political bias. Banks point to regulators. Regulators cite the law. Responsibility dissolves.

And yet, there are moments when the chain is consciously redesigned. Some authorities have begun to embed feedback mechanisms, reviewing licence data and market behaviour to adjust guidance. These efforts recognise that the chain is not fixed. It can be tuned. The relay can be slowed, accelerated, or rerouted.

The motif returns here as choice. In a relay, runners decide how to pass. Too fast and the baton drops. Too slow and the race is lost. Sanctions designers face an analogous trade-off. Speed delivers shock. Care delivers control. The chain mediates between them.

The sharpened test that emerges is practical. When a sanction is announced, can its architects trace, in advance, how it will be interpreted at each link? Can they anticipate where fear will amplify and where ambiguity will stall? The answer determines whether pressure aligns with purpose or dissipates into noise. The chain will always exist. The question is whether it is acknowledged and governed, or left to run on instinct alone.

Seeing sanctions as systems, not events

In October 2017, a policy aide seconded to the European External Action Service opened a spreadsheet that made no reference to geopolitics. It tracked delayed payments to hospitals and aid agencies operating in Yemen. The data came from humanitarian partners in Sana'a and Aden, collated by the Office for the Coordination of Humanitarian Affairs. The numbers were stark. According to OCHA's 2017 financial tracking, fewer than half of approved humanitarian transactions were settling within agreed timeframes. The sanctions regime aimed at armed actors was formally unchanged. The suffering was not. Something in the machinery was misfiring.

The paradox was familiar but rarely confronted. Sanctions are announced as decisions, often dramatic ones, tied to dates and statements. Their effects, however, unfold over months and years, shaped by reactions, adaptations, and frictions that no communiqué can capture. A measure intended to apply pressure can lose force even as its human cost rises. The system weakens while harm intensifies. That should not happen. It does.

Sanctions behave like systems, not switches.

The thesis follows directly. Treating sanctions as one-off events blinds designers to feedback, delay, and adaptation. Treating them as systems reveals why they often under-perform strategically while over-performing in harm. The difference lies not in moral intent, but in institutional design.

Systems thinking begins with an observation that is deceptively simple. Outcomes emerge from interactions, not instructions. In the sanctions context, the instruction is the legal measure. The interactions occur among banks, firms, regulators, aid agencies, and affected populations. Each adjusts behaviour in response to perceived risk and opportunity. The aggregate result is rarely linear.

Consider the Yemen case. The European Union and the United Nations maintained targeted sanctions against individuals linked to the conflict. Humanitarian exemptions were explicit. And yet banks, facing complex counterterrorism rules and past penalties, retreated. Payments slowed. Fuel imports faltered. Aid agencies reported increased costs and delays. Observe the gap between rule and result. Name it systemic drift. Explain that incentives at one node—bank risk committees—overrode intentions set elsewhere. The consequence was diminished leverage over armed actors and amplified suffering among civilians.

The policy aide did not propose scrapping sanctions. She proposed measurement. Her argument was procedural rather than ideological. If sanctions were meant to influence behaviour, their designers needed timely indicators of whether that influence was occurring and at what cost. She worked with colleagues to build a review loop linking humanitarian transaction data, licensing approvals, and market signals to periodic policy reassessment. The mechanism resembled a thermostat more than a switch. Adjust, observe, adjust again.

The image matters. A thermostat does not abandon heating when a room warms. It modulates. Without feedback, systems oscillate or fail.

The absence of such feedback has long plagued sanctions regimes. Political announcements generate attention; maintenance does not. Once imposed, measures persist by inertia. Review processes, where they exist, often focus on compliance rather than consequence. The result is what systems theorists call goal displacement. The metric of success becomes enforcement activity rather than behavioural change.

A second example sharpens the point. After the re-imposition of United States sanctions on Iran in May 2018, European governments sought to preserve legitimate trade. The Instrument in Support of Trade Exchanges, announced in January 2019 in Paris, was designed to facilitate humanitarian and permitted transactions. On paper, it addressed the problem. In practice, it moved little. Banks declined to participate. By 2020, INSTEX had processed only a handful of transactions. Observe the mismatch. Name it architectural failure. Explain that without alignment of incentives across the system, a new component cannot correct systemic fear. The consequence was symbolic relief without material effect.

These failures are not anomalies. They are predictable outcomes of treating sanctions as static decisions imposed on dynamic environments. Systems resist. Actors adapt. Feedback loops, whether designed or not, shape trajectories.

The language of systems clarifies several recurring puzzles. Why do sanctions sometimes lose effectiveness over time? Because targets adapt and networks reroute. Why does harm persist even after exemptions are issued? Because compliance cultures remember penalties longer than promises. Why do similar measures yield different outcomes across regions? Because institutional contexts differ.

A system is defined not only by its rules, but by its delays. In sanctions, delay is endemic. There is delay between designation and market response, between harm and reporting, between reporting and policy adjustment. Each delay dulls responsiveness. By the time humanitarian data reaches decision-makers, conditions on the ground may have shifted again. Without formalised loops, information arrives too late or not at all.

The aide's feedback proposal faced resistance. Some colleagues worried it would politicise humanitarian data. Others feared it would signal weakness. Still, a pilot went ahead. Review meetings incorporated transaction metrics and field reports. In cases where harm was clearly rising without corresponding pressure, guidance was clarified or licences broadened. Where pressure appeared to erode, designations were adjusted. The system did not become humane overnight. It became legible.

Legibility is a form of power.

Systems thinking also reframes accountability. When sanctions are treated as events, responsibility is pinned to the moment of decision. When treated as systems, responsibility extends to maintenance. Designers are accountable not only for what they impose, but for what they fail to adjust. This challenges institutional habits. Maintenance work is quieter, less visible, and less rewarded.

A credible limitation must be faced. Not all feedback is reliable, and not all harms can be mitigated without eroding pressure. Humanitarian data is partial. Targets may manipulate narratives. Excessive responsiveness risks signalling fragility. These concerns are real. They do not justify blindness. They argue for disciplined feedback, not its absence.

A comparison illustrates the balance. In South Africa during the 1980s, sanctions interacted with domestic mobilisation in ways that amplified pressure on the apartheid regime. The system's feedback—international divestment, domestic protest, diplomatic isolation—reinforced itself. In Iraq during the 1990s, comprehensive sanctions generated humanitarian catastrophe without producing political concession. Feedback existed, but adjustment was slow and contested. The difference was not intent. It was system design and responsiveness.

Metrics matter here. Studies by the World Bank and academic researchers in the early 2000s documented declines in child mortality only after sanctions regimes incorporated oil-for-food mechanisms. The harm had been measurable long before. Adjustment lagged. The thermostat was installed late.

The motif returns when considering enforcement. Enforcement agencies often measure success by actions taken: fines imposed, entities designated, guidance issued. These are inputs, not outcomes. A system perspective demands outcome metrics: behavioural change, conflict de-escalation, humanitarian access. These are harder to measure and easier to dispute. They are nonetheless essential.

Systems also contain reinforcing loops that designers may not anticipate. Over-compliance by banks reinforces caution by peers. Media coverage of penalties amplifies fear. Fear constrains activity beyond legal requirements. The loop tightens. Breaking it requires credible signals that precision will be protected. Without such signals, exhortations to "use exemptions" ring hollow.

The policy aide's work underscores a broader point. Seeing sanctions as systems shifts the locus of skill from declaration to design. It privileges monitoring over messaging. It demands humility about control and attentiveness to emergence. These qualities sit uneasily with the politics of pressure, yet they determine whether pressure works.

The thermostat image appears again when sanctions are lifted. Removal is not a mirror of imposition. Systems do not reset instantly. Relationships must be rebuilt. Trust must be restored. Without deliberate unwinding, relief lags. Iran's post-2016 experience showed how deeply embedded compliance habits can blunt political deals. Sanctions ended on paper; the system remained cold.

The sharpened choice facing sanctions architects is therefore practical. They can continue to treat measures as events—announce, enforce, move on—and accept recurrent cycles of under-performance and harm. Or they can invest in system design: feedback loops, outcome metrics, and adjustment mechanisms that acknowledge complexity without surrendering intent. The test is not whether sanctions are imposed, but whether they are governed.

The birth of the sanctions architect

On a wet Tuesday in November 2014, a senior associate at a City law firm sat revising a boilerplate clause she had amended dozens of times before. The client was a multinational commodities trader headquartered in London; the trigger was the European Union's sectoral sanctions against Russia adopted that July. The clause concerned termination rights if performance became unlawful. It was routine work, measured in billable hours. Yet as she compared drafts, she realised that her language would determine whether suppliers in Latvia could continue shipping components to plants in Kazakhstan, whether insurers in Zurich would keep cover in place, whether banks would finance inventory already afloat in the Baltic. One sentence. Many consequences. She paused. This mattered.

Sanctions rarely announce the identities of those who give them shape. Press statements cite governments and agencies. Legal texts bear institutional seals. The paradox is that the most consequential choices are often made by professionals whose names never appear. A commercial lawyer editing a contract, a risk officer adjusting a policy, a programmer calibrating a filter. These are not executioners of policy; they are designers of possibility. The sanctions architect emerges at precisely this junction.

A quiet role forms.

The thesis is clear. A sanctions architect is not defined by formal authority, but by functional influence. This professional identity arose as sanctions migrated from discrete prohibitions to pervasive systems, embedding political intent into private governance. As finance and law became the primary vectors of pressure, those who structured transactions acquired power over outcomes that once belonged to states alone.

Observe the conditions that produced this shift. Financial sanctions expanded rapidly after the early 2000s, particularly through banking and contractual mechanisms. As seen earlier, pressure moved inward, from borders to balance sheets. Name the effect: privatised enforcement. Explain that governments increasingly relied on firms to interpret and apply rules, incentivised by penalties rather than directives. The consequence was a diffusion of discretion into roles not traditionally associated with foreign policy.

The lawyer in London had not sought this role. She had trained in mergers and acquisitions, prized for her precision and speed. Sanctions entered her practice as risk. Clients demanded clauses that allowed them to exit deals without breaching the law. Each iteration became more cautious. Termination triggers widened. Representations grew more stringent. Counterparties pushed back. Negotiations stalled. Supply chains shifted. The drafting table became a site of geopolitics.

This dynamic was not unique. After the United States and the European Union tightened sanctions against Iran in 2012, major energy firms rewrote contracts to include expansive sanctions compliance warranties. According to analysis by the International Bar Association in 2013, force majeure clauses citing sanctions increased markedly in cross-border contracts involving the Middle East. The language varied, but the pattern held. Legal precaution reshaped commercial behaviour before regulators intervened.

The sanctions architect, then, is characterised by three features. First, proximity to operational decisions. Second, discretion under uncertainty. Third, asymmetric accountability. These professionals decide how rules are applied, yet rarely receive feedback on broader effects. Their success is measured by avoidance of breach, not by alignment with policy goals.

The blueprint motif fits here. Architects draw plans that others inhabit. They do not live in the building, but their decisions determine how light enters and where walls constrain. Sanctions architects draft frameworks within which others move. The blueprint is legal text, policy, or code. Once built, it is difficult to alter.

The London lawyer's realisation deepened when a client asked for advice on exiting a long-term supply contract with a firm in eastern Europe whose shareholders included a newly designated individual. The law did not require termination. The risk committee did. Her advice would determine whether dozens of subcontracts unravelled. She advised exit. The client complied. The designation had travelled far from its source.

Name the phenomenon: anticipatory compliance. Explain that professionals often act ahead of explicit prohibition to shield institutions from future exposure. The consequence is that sanctions bite harder and wider than intended.

This anticipatory behaviour is rational. Enforcement penalties are severe and retrospective. Guidance is often ambiguous. Courts defer to regulators. Under these conditions, caution dominates. But rationality at the individual level does not guarantee coherence at the system level. The architect optimises locally; the structure may fail globally.

A second named example illustrates the breadth of the role. In March 2012, when SWIFT disconnected Iranian banks, the decision rested on European regulations. Yet the operational criteria—how to identify affected messages, how to manage false positives—were set by technologists in Belgium. Their parameters determined which transactions failed and which slipped through. Engineers became architects. The blueprint was code.

This expansion of the architect's domain complicates accountability. Lawyers answer to clients. Engineers answer to managers. Compliance officers answer to regulators. No one answers directly for systemic harm. The diffusion is structural.

A credible limitation must be acknowledged. Not every professional touched by sanctions wields meaningful influence. Many roles are constrained, procedural, or purely executory. Moreover, some architects operate within tight guidance that leaves little room for discretion. Recognising the category does not romanticise it. It delineates responsibility where it exists.

The emergence of the sanctions architect also reflects a cultural shift within institutions. Sanctions knowledge became a valued specialism. Firms recruited former regulators. Training programmes proliferated. A shared epistemic community formed, trading interpretations and typologies. This professionalisation brought rigour. It also entrenched norms that prioritised defensibility over nuance.

Metrics reveal the scale. By 2019, major international banks were spending hundreds of millions annually on sanctions compliance, according to estimates by the Institute of International Finance. The investment signalled seriousness. It also amplified the power of those designing internal controls. Decisions once marginal became central.

The blueprint motif returns when considering moral awareness. Architects rarely see occupants. The London lawyer did not meet factory workers affected by contract terminations. The engineer did not speak to families waiting on remittances. Distance is built into the role. Some practitioners push against it, seeking information beyond their immediate remit. Others accept it as necessary insulation.

The birth of this identity has implications beyond description. It challenges the idea that sanctions are impersonal tools. They are assembled by people making trade-offs under pressure. Each clause, threshold, or parameter encodes a judgment about acceptable risk and acceptable harm.

A third example underscores the point. In 2018, a European bank's compliance team decided to exit all relationships involving a sanctioned jurisdiction, despite humanitarian exemptions. The decision exceeded legal requirements. It was justified internally as prudence. Aid agencies protested. Regulators expressed concern but imposed no penalty. The architects of that policy were mid-level managers responding to incentives. Their choice reshaped access to finance for an entire sector.

This raises the sharpened trade-off at the heart of the role. Sanctions architects can design for maximum insulation or for calibrated engagement. Insulation minimises institutional risk. Calibration preserves policy intent and reduces harm. Both cannot be maximised simultaneously.

The question that closes this inquiry is practical rather than rhetorical. As sanctions continue to rely on private infrastructure, will those who design the blueprints recognise their authorship? Awareness does not eliminate constraint, but it alters posture. Acknowledging the role invites reflection on how discretion is exercised and how systems might be adjusted without abandoning purpose. The sanctions architect is already at work. The choice is whether to remain invisible or to accept the responsibilities that visibility brings.

Chapter 2
Building Payment Chokepoints

At 10.03 a.m. on 1 March 2022, a short operational message circulated inside a cooperative headquartered outside Brussels. It was not addressed to the public. It was not drafted for history. It instructed staff at SWIFT to begin implementing disconnection measures against a defined set of Russian banks, following days of emergency diplomacy after the invasion of Ukraine. In the operations rooms, screens filled with identifiers rather than headlines. There was no cheering, no sense of triumph. There was tension, and a quiet awareness that once the switch was thrown, it would not only slow tanks but also stop salaries, tuition payments, and remittances far from any battlefield.

SWIFT had spent decades insisting on its neutrality. It was a messenger, not a judge; a utility, not an instrument of power. And yet, when the decision came, it was SWIFT that sat at the fulcrum. Not armies. Not navies. A messaging system.

This chapter begins at that point of inversion, where infrastructure designed to facilitate trust becomes a mechanism of exclusion. It follows how payment chokepoints are deliberately built, calibrated, and defended by people who rarely think of themselves as coercive actors, even as they are asked to implement some of the most consequential measures in modern statecraft.

The rise of financial sanctions shifted attention from goods to flows, but payment systems gave that shift teeth. Banks can trade without ships; they cannot trade without settlement. Messaging standards, correspondent accounts, screening software, and risk policies form the narrow passages through which money must pass. Close or constrict those passages, and pressure radiates outward with remarkable speed. This is not incidental. It is design.

The first architects of payment chokepoints were not ideologues. They were technocrats, lawyers, and regulators wrestling with practical questions. How could pressure be applied without imposing comprehensive embargoes that harmed allies as much as targets? How could enforcement be scaled in a globalised economy where transactions move faster than inspections? The answer, gradually, was to move upstream. If money could not move, trade would stall on its own.

SWIFT's transformation into a pressure point captures the logic. Founded in the 1970s as a cooperative owned by its member banks, SWIFT standardised financial messaging to reduce error and increase speed. Its codes were boring by design. Neutrality was not a slogan; it was a prerequisite for adoption. For decades, SWIFT resisted political entanglement, arguing that its legitimacy depended on universal trust.

That position became harder to sustain as sanctions regimes grew more ambitious. By the early 2010s, policymakers recognised that excluding banks from SWIFT access could achieve what asset freezes and trade bans often could not: immediate isolation. The Iran disconnection of March 2012 was the turning point. It was legally grounded in European regulation, but operationally unprecedented. Inside SWIFT, staff worried openly about precedent. If one group of banks could be cut off under political pressure, what would stop fragmentation? Would alternative networks proliferate? Would trust erode?

Those fears never fully dissipated. They sit at the heart of every subsequent disconnection debate. Yet the tool proved irresistible. When Russian banks were excluded a decade later, the question was no longer whether SWIFT could be used as leverage, but how far and how fast.

Building a chokepoint does not end with a headline decision. It begins a cascade of secondary design choices. Which institutions are named? Are subsidiaries included? How are new messages filtered? What grace periods apply? Each choice shapes behaviour. Narrow measures can be evaded; broad ones can shock entire markets. The technocrats drafting exclusion protocols understand this. They balance precision against urgency, knowing that either extreme carries risk.

Beyond SWIFT, the chokepoint logic deepens inside banks themselves. Once a new sanctions package is announced, attention shifts from public statements to internal systems. Screening teams ingest updated lists. Data specialists recalibrate name-matching algorithms. Thresholds are tightened or loosened. A change from 85 per cent to 90 per cent similarity may sound trivial. In practice, it can double the number of alerts. The difference between a weapons broker and a paediatric supplier can hinge on a diacritic.

One data specialist recalls being asked, late one evening after a major designation, to "make it safer by morning". Safer meant fewer misses. It also meant more false positives. The models complied. Overnight, transaction queues lengthened. Relationship managers complained. Customers waited. The algorithm had no sense of urgency or innocence. It followed the rule.

This is where payment chokepoints become human. Decisions taken to protect institutions from regulatory risk translate directly into lived experience. A tightened filter does not announce itself as policy. It manifests as silence: a payment that does not arrive, an invoice left unpaid, a message that loops back with no explanation. The help-desk becomes a confessional. Staff trained to explain processes become counsellors, absorbing frustration they did not create and cannot resolve.

The chokepoint widens again at the level of correspondent banking. Global finance depends on a web of relationships linking local banks to international clearing institutions. Maintaining those links requires trust and constant due diligence. Under sanctions pressure, that trust frays. Risk managers reassess marginal relationships. One compliance chief, after a sanctions enforcement action in a neighbouring jurisdiction, decided to sever ties with a small foreign bank whose controls were deemed inadequate. The decision complied with no formal requirement. It was precautionary. The consequence was immediate. Businesses in the affected country lost access to cross-border payments. Remittances slowed. Communities were cut off from the financial system not by law, but by fear.

This phenomenon—de-risking—has been documented extensively by the World Bank and the Financial Stability Board since the mid-

2010s. It illustrates how payment chokepoints multiply beyond their designers' intent. When penalties are severe and guidance ambiguous, institutions rationally retreat. Each retreat narrows the passage further. What begins as targeted pressure becomes systemic exclusion.

The cumulative effect is what makes payment chokepoints so potent and so dangerous. They operate through aggregation. No single decision is decisive. Together, they constrict flow. The image is hydraulic. Pressure builds where channels narrow. Release valves exist in theory—humanitarian exemptions, general licences—but reaching them requires navigation through layers of caution.

This chapter moves through those layers deliberately. It begins with SWIFT because it sits at the symbolic centre of financial connectivity. It then descends into the quieter machinery of bank screening, where code and policy intersect. It widens again to correspondent risk, where strategic fear reshapes geography. Finally, it reaches the point where abstraction meets domestic reality: the stalled remittance, the unpaid fee, the family waiting at a kitchen table for money that should have arrived days ago.

What binds these scenes is not malice but design. Payment chokepoints are built by professionals solving immediate problems within constrained systems. They rarely see the full arc. The technocrat worries about precedent. The data specialist worries about misses. The risk manager worries about penalties. Each worry is legitimate. Together, they produce outcomes no single actor intended.

The modern relevance is unavoidable. As geopolitical rivalry intensifies and financial systems become more interconnected, the temptation to use payment infrastructure as leverage grows. Digital currencies, alternative messaging systems, and regional clearing arrangements are often discussed as escape routes. Their very discussion is evidence of how central the chokepoint has become. Once infrastructure is weaponised, others will seek to route around it.

Yet the question is not whether payment chokepoints exist. They do. The question is how consciously they are designed and governed. Are they treated as blunt instruments, tightened reflexively in moments of crisis? Or are they understood as delicate mechanisms requiring calibration, feedback, and restraint?

This chapter does not offer a single answer. It offers a way of seeing. By following the people who build and maintain payment chokepoints, it reveals how financial pressure is made operational and where it leaks. It shows why a messaging utility can become a strategic lever, how an algorithmic tweak can stall a hospital order, and why a risk decision in one city can strand a community in another.

The reader is left not with certainty, but with sharpened attention. Every payment that moves—or fails to—has passed through human hands, rules, and judgments. To understand sanctions as they now function, one must understand how those chokepoints are built, tightened, and, sometimes, quietly regretted.

How SWIFT became a pressure tool

On 17 March 2012, in La Hulpe outside Brussels, the board of SWIFT received formal notification that it must disconnect designated Iranian banks from its messaging services. The legal basis was an EU regulation adopted days earlier; the operational deadline was immediate. SWIFT complied. Within hours, payment confirmations stopped arriving in Tehran. Oil cargoes continued to move, but the money did not. A cooperative built to transmit trust had been instructed to interrupt it.

A messaging system had become a switch.

The transformation was neither sudden nor inevitable. For four decades, SWIFT had insisted—credibly—that it was neutral plumbing. Founded in 1973 by banks seeking to replace error-prone telexes, it provided standardised messages, not judgement. It moved instructions, not funds. Its legitimacy rested on universality. Everyone could connect; no one was excluded for political reasons.

That stance was not philosophical. It was operational. Fragment the network and its value collapses.

The thesis that follows is exact. SWIFT became a pressure tool because financial sanctions migrated upstream into infrastructure, and because technocrats learned that denying access to shared systems could achieve effects no embargo could match. The consequence was leverage of extraordinary reach, accompanied by fears—voiced early and often—that the very system being used would fracture under the strain.

Observe the early pressure. After the attacks of September 2001, the United States Treasury sought faster access to financial data to track terrorist financing. SWIFT's message archives became a focal point. The Terrorist Finance Tracking Program, revealed publicly in 2006, strained SWIFT's claim to neutrality but stopped short of exclusion. Access was conditional, contested, and closely supervised. The system bent; it did not break. The switch remained off.

The decisive shift came when policymakers realised that exclusion itself could be policy. This required a conceptual leap. If SWIFT was merely a messenger, how could it deny service? The answer lay in law. SWIFT is incorporated in Belgium and subject to EU regulation. When EU law prohibited providing financial messaging services to named entities, neutrality yielded to compliance. The observation is stark. Infrastructure obeys jurisdiction. Name it legal capture. Explain that global systems are still anchored somewhere. The consequence is that political decisions at the centre can reconfigure networks at the edge.

The Iran case tested this logic. For months before March 2012, diplomats debated whether SWIFT disconnection would be excessive. Inside SWIFT, technologists mapped scenarios. How many banks? Which message types? What about false positives? They worried about collateral effects and precedent. Once done, could it be undone? The fears were not academic. Alternative messaging networks had existed before. If major users lost confidence, they might revive them.

Still, the instruction came. The implementation was precise. SWIFT identified Bank Identifier Codes associated with designated Iranian institutions and blocked their ability to send or receive messages. Correspondent banks followed suit. Letters of credit failed. According to the International Energy Agency, Iranian oil exports fell sharply later that year, though causality was shared with other measures. The pressure was undeniable. So was the lesson.

The switch worked.

A decade later, the same logic reappeared under far greater scrutiny. After Russia's invasion of Ukraine in February 2022, calls to disconnect Russian banks from SWIFT escalated rapidly. Governments debated scope and sequencing. Some feared escalation; others feared delay. Inside SWIFT, teams rehearsed contingency plans developed years earlier but never expected to use at scale. On 1 March 2022, the first disconnections began. More followed.

The technocrats involved were acutely aware of the risks. Russia was not Iran. Its integration into global finance was deeper; its retaliation capacity greater. Would exclusion accelerate fragmentation? Would parallel systems—Russia's SPFS or China's CIPS—gain traction? These were not rhetorical questions. They shaped implementation choices. Only certain banks were disconnected initially. Energy payments were treated cautiously. The switch was flicked, then held.

Observe the pattern. In both cases, SWIFT's role was not to choose targets but to operationalise choice. Name it infrastructural enforcement. Explain that power accrues to those who control gateways, even when they disclaim intent. The consequence is that technologists become custodians of coercion.

The internal work of making exclusion possible is often misunderstood. It is not a single command but a bundle of protocols. Access conditions must be defined. Lists must be maintained. Appeals must be handled. Error rates must be minimised. Each task embeds judgement. A too-broad filter risks blocking permitted messages; a too-narrow one invites evasion. The technocrats drafting these rules are not merely executing law. They are shaping its effect.

Metrics make this visible. After the 2012 Iran disconnection, SWIFT reported a spike in operational queries from banks seeking clarification on message failures. Each query represented uncertainty translating into caution. In 2022, similar patterns emerged, amplified by scale. Banks froze exposures beyond those required. Market liquidity thinned. The system reacted to the switch by narrowing its own channels.

This narrowing is the motif that binds the story. SWIFT disconnection does not stop trade directly. It narrows the communicative channel through which trade is settled. Pressure builds upstream. The narrowing is deliberate, but its spread is emergent.

A credible limitation deserves attention. SWIFT exclusion is neither total nor irreversible. Messages can be routed through intermediaries; alternative networks can be built. Indeed, after 2014, Russia invested in domestic messaging. China expanded CIPS. These developments complicate the leverage. Yet they do not negate it. Alternatives lack scale and interoperability. The value of SWIFT lies in its ubiquity. Fragmentation remains costly.

Moreover, overuse carries risk. Each deployment of the switch invites others to hedge. Technocrats know this. It informs their caution. The fear of system fracture is not sentimental. It is empirical. Network value declines with division.

The role of technocrats here is distinctive. They are not elected, yet they operate at the hinge of policy and infrastructure. They negotiate access conditions with regulators, draft exclusion protocols, and model downstream effects. Their language is technical, their stakes geopolitical. They speak of resilience and redundancy while understanding that both can undermine leverage.

The second echo of the motif appears in reversal. Once the switch is used, turning it back is harder than expected. Reconnection requires trust restoration. Systems do not forget exclusions. After partial delistings in both Iran and Russia cases, banks hesitated. The channel remained narrowed. Pressure lingered beyond intent.

The sharpened choice at the close is unavoidable. SWIFT can be treated as an exceptional lever, pulled rarely and with restraint, or as a routine instrument of pressure. The former preserves network integrity but limits policy agility. The latter maximises leverage but accelerates fragmentation. Technocrats stand between these options, translating political urgency into infrastructural reality.

The story of how SWIFT became a pressure tool is not one of capture or betrayal. It is a story of jurisdiction, design, and consequence. A system built to connect was asked to exclude. It complied, carefully, aware that each use of the switch changes the circuit itself.

Designing bank screening rules

At 11.47 p.m. on 6 April 2018, a sanctions alert landed in the operations inbox of a global bank's compliance analytics team in Canary Wharf. The United States Treasury had just announced a tranche of new designations linked to Russia, including several major corporates. Markets were still open in Asia. Payments were already in flight. The message from senior management was terse: tighten the filters before morning. The data specialist on call opened the configuration panel that governed name-matching thresholds across millions of daily transactions. One number stood between continuity and interruption.

Small numbers decide big outcomes.

Sanctions screening inside banks is often imagined as a mechanical exercise: lists in, matches out. The reality is closer to engineering under uncertainty. Screening systems do not discover illegality; they infer risk from imperfect signals. They compare names, addresses, ownership chains, and transaction patterns against evolving lists, using algorithms that balance sensitivity against noise. The thesis is precise. Bank screening rules are design choices, not neutral safeguards, and marginal adjustments can reshape the real-world impact of sanctions more decisively than public law.

Observe the context in which these choices are made. A major designation triggers immediate fear of misses. Enforcement penalties are retrospective and severe. Guidance is partial. Time is short. Name this condition defensive optimisation. Explain that institutions prioritise avoiding false negatives—letting a prohibited transaction through—over reducing false positives. The consequence is predictable: systems err on the side of blockage.

The data specialist in London understood the trade-off. Her models used fuzzy matching to compare customer names against sanctions lists. A similarity score of 85 per cent had been the escalation threshold. Raising it to 90 would catch more variants, transliterations, and misspellings. It would also flag many legitimate parties with common names. She ran simulations. Alert volumes doubled. Processing times lengthened. Relationship managers would complain. Hospitals would wait. She raised the threshold anyway.

That night's decision illustrates how screening rules translate policy into experience. The algorithm did not know the difference between a weapons broker and a paediatric supplier. It knew only similarity scores. Humans supplied the intent; machines executed it. The distinction matters because the harm does not arise from malice but from configuration.

Screening systems grew in prominence as sanctions lists expanded. After 9/11, banks invested heavily in automated monitoring. Vendors offered increasingly sophisticated tools, promising precision through data enrichment and machine learning. Yet even the most advanced systems require parameters. Thresholds, weights, and escalation rules must be set. These are not dictated by regulators. They are chosen.

A named example makes this concrete. Following the 2014 BNP Paribas settlement with US authorities, which resulted in a penalty of nearly $9 billion, banks across Europe reviewed their screening programmes. Internal audits recommended tighter thresholds and broader watchlists. According to a 2015 survey by the Institute of

International Finance, compliance alert volumes increased by more than 30 per cent at several major banks. The numbers reflected decisions, not discoveries. More alerts did not mean more wrongdoing. They meant more caution.

The motif here is the dial. Screening rules operate like dials, not switches. Turn one slightly and the system's behaviour changes materially. Turn several and the effect compounds. The dial is rarely turned back.

Banks justify these settings through governance. Committees approve risk appetites. Policies codify thresholds. Vendors are instructed. Yet governance does not eliminate discretion; it distributes it. The data specialist implements what the committee authorises. The committee relies on metrics the system produces. Circularity ensues.

The human cost appears downstream. In 2019, humanitarian organisations working in Syria reported frequent payment delays despite holding valid licences. Banks cited screening hits. Names of clinics resembled those of designated entities. Appeals took weeks. According to reports by the Norwegian Refugee Council that year, some aid deliveries were postponed because funds had not cleared. The law permitted the payments. The system stalled them.

Translate abstraction into behaviour. A transaction is flagged. An analyst reviews it against guidance. Uncertainty persists. Escalation follows. The clock runs. No one wants to approve wrongly. Delay becomes the safest option. Multiply this across thousands of transactions and the dial's effect becomes systemic.

A second example underscores the point. In 2020, as the COVID-19 pandemic strained health systems, several banks reported spikes in screening alerts linked to medical suppliers shipping to sanctioned jurisdictions. Names of manufacturers overlapped with those of designated firms in other sectors. Temporary guidance was issued by regulators to reassure banks. Screening thresholds, however, remained unchanged. Payments slowed. Equipment arrived late. The mismatch between policy intent and system behaviour was stark.

These outcomes are not accidents. They follow from the incentive structure. Screening teams are rewarded for compliance, not for enabling lawful activity. Misses attract penalties; blocks attract complaints. One risk dominates.

The credible limitation must be stated. Screening rules are not arbitrary. They catch real threats. Weapons dealers and proliferators do exploit name variants and shell entities. Looser thresholds would increase successful evasion. Precision is difficult. This is not an argument for laxity. It is an argument for recognising cost.

Reconciling this limitation requires acknowledging asymmetry. The harm of a miss is concentrated on the institution and regulator. The harm of a block is diffused across customers and communities. Systems respond to concentrated risk more forcefully than to dispersed harm. The dial turns towards caution.

Technological sophistication does not dissolve the problem. Machine learning models promise context-aware screening, but they depend on training data and governance. In practice, many banks constrain such models to avoid explainability issues. Regulators demand transparency. Simpler rules persist. Thresholds remain blunt.

The motif returns when thresholds are adjusted again. After the initial shock of the April 2018 designations, some banks quietly relaxed settings as alert backlogs grew unmanageable. The dial moved back a notch. Yet few returned to pre-announcement levels. The system remembered the scare. Memory matters.

Inside screening teams, moral awareness varies. Some analysts push for nuance, flagging patterns that suggest humanitarian use. Others stick rigidly to protocol. Training emphasises procedure. Time pressures discourage reflection. The architecture of work shapes judgement.

Metrics can reveal the trade-offs. Average alert resolution times increase as thresholds tighten. Customer attrition rises. Correspondent banks reassess relationships. These indicators are often monitored separately, owned by different departments. Few institutions integrate them into a single view. Systems thinking is rare inside silos.

The sharpened choice that emerges is operational. Banks can continue to design screening rules primarily to avoid worst-case regulatory outcomes, accepting routine collateral damage. Or they can invest in governance that treats thresholds as policy levers, subject to review based on observed effects. This does not require weakening sanctions. It requires acknowledging that algorithms are instruments of judgement, not substitutes for it.

The dial will always exist. Someone will always turn it. The question is whether those decisions are made in the dark, or with sight of what they block as well as what they protect.

Managing correspondent banking risk

In August 2016, in a glass-walled office overlooking the River Main in Frankfurt, the chief compliance officer of a mid-sized European bank signed a termination letter. The counterparty was a small commercial bank in the Horn of Africa, connected through a correspondent account that cleared euro transactions. The trigger was not a breach, nor a designation. It was a sanctions scare: a press report suggesting that one of the African bank's clients might have indirect links to a sanctioned individual. No regulator had called. No rule had changed. Still, the relationship ended. Within weeks, remittance flows from diaspora communities in Germany slowed to a trickle. Entire towns felt it.

One decision. Many lives downstream.

Correspondent banking sits at the quiet heart of global finance. It allows a local bank to access foreign currencies and payment systems by relying on a partner with broader reach. Without correspondents, banks become islands. With them, they are bridges. The thesis here is exact and uncomfortable. Decisions about correspondent banking relationships, made by risk managers under sanctions pressure, have become one of the most powerful and least visible instruments of financial exclusion, often creating de facto sanctions far beyond any official list.

Observe the structural context. After the expansion of financial sanctions and the escalation of enforcement penalties in the 2010s, banks reassessed their exposure to cross-border risk. Correspondent relationships, especially with smaller or higher-risk jurisdictions, came under scrutiny. Name the process: de-risking. Explain that institutions choose to withdraw from relationships perceived as costly to monitor relative to their revenue. The consequence is not targeted pressure on bad actors, but wholesale retreat from regions and sectors.

The compliance chief in Frankfurt faced a familiar calculation. The correspondent account generated modest fees. Monitoring it required enhanced due diligence, periodic site visits, and constant screening. A single lapse could expose the bank to regulatory action. The expected value of continuation was low; the downside unbounded. Fear dominated arithmetic. She cut the bridge.

Fear is efficient.

Correspondent risk management is often framed as prudence. Regulators encourage banks to understand their partners' controls and customer bases. In principle, this promotes integrity. In practice, it incentivises withdrawal. A 2015 report by the World Bank documented a global decline in correspondent banking relationships, particularly affecting Africa, the Caribbean, and parts of the Middle East. The timing coincided with heightened sanctions enforcement. Correlation does not prove causation, but the alignment is telling.

The motif of the bridge clarifies what is lost. A correspondent account is not merely a technical arrangement; it is a conduit for trade, aid, and family support. When a bridge is removed, alternatives are scarce. Informal channels fill the gap, often with higher cost and lower transparency. The system does not become safer. It becomes darker.

The Frankfurt case is not isolated. In 2014, after a major US enforcement action against a European bank for sanctions violations, several global banks curtailed correspondent services to Somali banks. The effect was immediate. Remittances from the Somali diaspora, estimated by the World Bank in 2016 at over $1.3 billion annually, faced disruption. Humanitarian agencies warned of knock-on effects. The sanctions regimes in question did not target Somalia's financial sector. The fear did.

Name the phenomenon: risk transmutation. Explain that sanctions risk aimed at specific behaviours mutates into geographic and sectoral exclusion when filtered through institutional incentives. The consequence is that compliance becomes indistinguishable from embargo.

Risk managers occupy an unenviable position. They are judged on avoidance. A clean audit is success. A relationship that never existed cannot breach. Their dashboards track exposures, alerts, and regulatory interactions. They rarely track social impact. This asymmetry shapes decisions.

The bridge motif appears again in internal discussions. Risk committees speak of "connecting risk". Each correspondent is a pathway through which unknown activity might flow. The language is hydraulic. Flow equals danger. The safest option is closure.

Yet this logic has limits. Not all relationships are equally risky, and not all withdrawals reduce harm. Blanket de-risking can undermine financial inclusion, push activity into unregulated channels, and erode the very transparency regulators seek. A 2018 Financial Stability Board report acknowledged these risks, urging banks to manage rather than avoid correspondent relationships. The guidance was measured. The incentives remained unchanged.

A second named example illustrates divergence. In 2019, a large UK bank chose to maintain correspondent ties with several West African institutions despite sanctions-related concerns. It invested in on-site audits, shared training, and transaction monitoring support. The costs were real. The relationships endured. Remittance flows continued. The bank accepted residual risk. This approach was not rewarded by markets, but it avoided exclusion. Precision replaced fear.

This counter-example matters. It shows that de-risking is not inevitable. It is a choice shaped by governance and culture. Some institutions treat correspondent banking as a strategic commitment; others treat it as a liability. The difference lies in how risk is priced and owned.

A credible limitation must be faced. Some correspondent relationships are genuinely untenable. Weak controls, opaque ownership, and hostile jurisdictions create risks that cannot be mitigated at reasonable cost. Withdrawal in such cases is defensible. The argument is not against exit per se, but against indiscriminate exit driven by sanctions anxiety rather than evidence.

Reconciling this limitation requires attention to thresholds. What level of residual risk is acceptable? Who decides? In many banks, the answer defaults to zero tolerance because accountability is individual while benefit is diffuse. The compliance chief bears the blame for a failure; no one bears credit for maintaining a lifeline.

Metrics can sharpen the picture. After correspondent withdrawals, transaction volumes drop sharply. Costs rise. Cash usage increases. These indicators are measurable. They are rarely fed back into risk assessments. The bridge collapses quietly.

The human dimension is hardest to ignore. When the Frankfurt bank severed ties, migrant workers struggled to send money home. School fees went unpaid. Medical expenses were deferred. These outcomes were not intended. They were foreseeable. The compliance chief knew remittances flowed through the account. She did not know the faces. Distance made the decision easier.

The motif returns one last time in restoration. Rebuilding correspondent relationships is arduous. Trust, once withdrawn, is slow to return. Even when sanctions ease, bridges remain down. Institutions remember fear longer than reassurance. The system ossifies.

The sharpened choice that closes this inquiry is institutional. Banks can continue to manage correspondent risk primarily through withdrawal, accepting the creation of de facto sanctions as collateral. Or they can invest in differentiated risk management that preserves critical links while isolating genuine threats. This choice does not abolish sanctions. It determines whether their force is channelled or indiscriminate. The bridge will stand or fall on decisions made far from those who depend on it.

Collateral damage in payment rails

On 14 February 2019, at 9.12 a.m. in Leicester, a help-desk specialist at a high-street bank answered a call that had already been transferred twice. The customer was a care worker sending £380 to her parents in Mogadishu. The transfer had been marked "pending" for eleven days. The system showed no error, only silence. The specialist searched the notes, saw the familiar internal tag—*sanctions review*—and felt the familiar tightening. There was nothing she could fix. She apologised anyway. The money was needed for insulin. It was Valentine's Day.

Payments move. People wait.

Financial sanctions are designed to apply pressure upstream, at institutions and networks. Their downstream effects are rarely mapped with equal care. Payment rails—the everyday channels that carry remittances, tuition fees, pensions, charity funds—become sites of unintended capture when chokepoints tighten. The thesis is direct. Collateral damage in payment rails is not an aberration but a systemic outcome of sanctions applied through private infrastructure, where fear, automation, and opacity intersect.

Observe the mechanics. A transaction enters the banking system, is screened, flagged, escalated, and paused. Name the phenomenon: procedural suspension. Explain that pauses accumulate when institutions prioritise certainty over speed. The consequence is delay without denial, a limbo that erodes trust and causes harm without leaving a traceable decision.

The help-desk specialist in Leicester had learned to recognise this limbo. She could see when a payment had not failed but had not moved. Her role was customer service, yet she became an interpreter of a system that spoke only in codes. She explained compliance reviews to callers who had never heard the term. She offered timelines she could not guarantee. Over time, callers stopped asking about process and began explaining need.

The kitchen table is where sanctions become legible. A family calculates whether to borrow. A student wonders if fees will post before the deadline. A charity delays a shipment. These are not marginal transactions. According to the World Bank, remittance flows to low- and middle-income countries reached $529 billion in 2018. Even small frictions scale.

The Leicester case was not unique. In 2017, after several global banks curtailed services to Somalia-linked corridors, UK money service businesses reported widespread delays. The UK Financial Conduct Authority acknowledged the issue in guidance that year, noting the tension between sanctions compliance and financial inclusion. Guidance did not move money. The rails remained clogged.

Translate abstraction into behaviour. Screening systems flag names common in certain regions. Analysts escalate. Supervisors request more documentation. Counterpart banks ask questions. Each step adds hours or days. No one intends harm. Harm accrues.

A second named example sharpens the point. In March 2020, as COVID-19 spread, a European charity attempted to transfer funds for protective equipment to a partner clinic in northwest Syria. The payment was lawful under existing humanitarian exemptions. It was nevertheless held by an intermediary bank for enhanced review. According to correspondence later shared with donors, the delay exceeded three weeks. Supplies arrived late. The exemption existed. The rail did not carry it.

Name the effect: exemption decay. Explain that permissions weaken as they pass through layers of risk management. The consequence is that lawful activity is treated as exceptional, requiring proof at every step, while prohibition is assumed.

The motif binding these scenes is the queue. Payments do not vanish; they queue. Queues are invisible to those who design systems and painfully visible to those who wait. The queue lengthens when thresholds tighten, when correspondent links shrink, when staff are overburdened. The queue is where policy meets time.

Help-desk staff live with the queue. Their scripts are thin. They cannot disclose internal flags. They are trained to de-escalate emotion, not to resolve cause. Over months, some develop coping strategies: offering empathy without hope, suggesting alternative channels they know are worse. A few keep informal lists of frequent callers. They become unofficial counsellors, absorbing distress generated elsewhere.

The systemic nature of the harm becomes clearer when patterns repeat across contexts. Tuition fees to sanctioned jurisdictions stall at the start of academic terms. Pensions sent to retirees abroad are delayed without explanation. Small charities see transfers returned after weeks with no reason given. These outcomes correlate with sanctions announcements, enforcement actions, and guidance updates. Timing matters.

A credible limitation must be acknowledged. Some payments should be stopped. Sanctions aim to prevent funds reaching prohibited actors. Screening catches real risks. Delays can avert diversion. This is true. Reconciling this limitation requires distinguishing necessary interruption from indiscriminate congestion. The queue grows not only because dangerous items are inspected, but because safe items are treated as suspect by default.

Evidence supports the distinction. A 2019 study by the Overseas Development Institute documented that humanitarian organisations faced payment delays primarily due to banks' internal risk aversion rather than legal prohibition. Where banks invested in specialised humanitarian desks, delays shortened. Where they did not, queues persisted. Design choices mattered.

The kitchen table returns in the Leicester family's story. After the twelfth day, the money was returned. No explanation. The sender used an informal hawala broker recommended by a friend. The funds arrived within hours. The bank lost the transaction. The system lost visibility. The sanction gained nothing.

Name the consequence: displacement. Explain that when formal rails clog, informal channels expand. The consequence is reduced transparency and control, undermining policy aims.

The help-desk specialist noticed this pattern. Customers stopped calling to ask when money would arrive. They called to close accounts. The bank's metrics showed attrition. No one linked it to sanctions. The queue was off the dashboard.

A third example underscores the breadth. In 2018, following heightened sanctions scrutiny, several European universities reported delayed tuition payments from students in certain regions. Students were enrolled, visas issued, classes begun. Fees sat pending. Administrative holds followed. Education became collateral. Universities appealed. Banks cited screening. The rail held.

The queue motif echoes again when payments finally clear. The relief is muted. Trust has already eroded. People plan around delay. They keep cash. They use intermediaries. The formal system becomes the slow option.

What makes this damage difficult to address is its invisibility. Sanctions are evaluated through macro indicators: export volumes, exchange rates, political concessions. Payment queues register nowhere. They are dispersed across households and desks. No single authority owns the problem.

Yet ownership exists in fragments. Banks choose thresholds. Regulators choose signals. Governments choose tools. Each can shorten or lengthen the queue. None does so deliberately for families at kitchen tables, yet their choices decide how long those families wait.

The sharpened trade-off is not moral but operational. Payment rails can be designed to distinguish better between risk and need, investing in specialised review, clearer guidance, and faster escalation for humanitarian and personal transfers. Or they can continue to absorb shock by default, letting queues grow because delay feels safer than error. The first option costs money and attention. The second costs trust.

The help-desk specialist still answers calls. She keeps a notepad with reminders: breathe, apologise, do not promise. She has learned that sanctions do not feel like pressure at the point of impact. They feel like waiting.

Chapter 3
Export Controls And Hidden Cargo

On a cold morning in February 2016, a shipping container sat unopened on the apron of Rotterdam's Maasvlakte terminal. Its paperwork was immaculate. The declared contents were industrial pumps, bound for a distributor in Central Asia. Nothing on the control list obviously applied. And yet a licensing officer in The Hague had placed the shipment on hold. The pumps, she suspected, could be repurposed for chemical processing. The end-user was opaque. The law was silent. The decision was hers, and the clock was running.

Export controls have always lived in this space between certainty and suspicion. They were once imagined as lists: enumerations of goods too dangerous to trade freely. If an item appeared on the list, it required a licence. If it did not, it moved. That logic suited a world of discrete technologies and clearly bounded industries. It no longer fits the world we inhabit.

This chapter opens at the moment when export controls ceased to be merely about goods and became instead about intent, capability, and design. The shift is subtle, technical, and profoundly consequential. Unlike financial sanctions, export controls rarely make headlines. They work in silence, through forms, definitions, and case-by-case judgement. Their power lies not in spectacle but in calibration.

The modern export control regime emerged from frustration. Static lists proved too easy to game and too blunt to guide. Technologies evolved faster than schedules could be updated. Dual-use items—civilian in appearance, military in application—multiplied. A valve designed for a pharmaceutical plant could also serve a weapons programme. A microchip for a consumer device could guide a missile. The line between benign and malign use blurred, and with it the adequacy of list-based control.

One response was conceptual. Control shifted from objects to strategies. Rather than asking only *what* was being shipped, authorities began to ask *to whom*, *for what purpose*, and *within which system*. This demanded a different kind of work. It required civil servants capable of redesigning licensing logic, not just administering it.

The chapter follows one such figure: a mid-career official tasked with overhauling a dual-use licensing scheme after a public scandal exposed its weaknesses. The law did not change. The definitions did. Thresholds were reinterpreted. Guidance was rewritten. Overnight, the same statute produced different outcomes. Pressure tightened without a single parliamentary vote.

This is a recurring theme. Export controls often exert their force not through new prohibitions but through reinterpretation. Definitions expand or contract. Risk indicators are weighted differently. What counts as "knowledge" of end-use is clarified. Each adjustment is technical. Each reshapes trade.

The frontline of this system is the licensing officer. These are not faceless bureaucrats. They are trained professionals reading shipping manifests, corporate registries, and intelligence summaries, often under time pressure and political scrutiny. Their desks accumulate borderline cases: medical imaging equipment for a sanctioned region; laboratory glassware for a university with mixed funding; spare parts for infrastructure in a conflict zone. The law offers criteria. It does not offer certainty.

One officer's struggle with a shipment of advanced diagnostic equipment illustrates the dilemma. The device could save lives. It could also be adapted for prohibited research. Denying the licence would delay treatment. Approving it might enable diversion. The officer consulted colleagues, reviewed end-user statements, requested additional assurances. Days passed. Industries adjusted. Hospitals waited. Decisions like this do not stay small. Repeated across sectors, they shape supply chains and investment patterns.

Export controls, then, are accumulative. Case-by-case decisions aggregate into structural effects. Manufacturers redesign products to fall below thresholds. Traders reroute shipments through third countries. Universities reconsider collaborations. None of this requires a new law. It requires consistent application of discretion.

That discretion has been transformed by data. Where earlier generations of officers relied on paper files and personal networks, today's analysts work with sprawling datasets. Customs records, shipping logs, corporate ownership databases, and satellite imagery are combined to map supply chains in near real time. This engineering of visibility has altered what is possible.

The chapter introduces a data analyst who uncovered a sophisticated diversion scheme by correlating spikes in niche exports with changes in corporate directorships across jurisdictions. The goods were not illegal per se. The pattern was. By revealing the hidden cargo routes, the analyst gave policymakers options short of blanket bans. Targeted pressure replaced broad restriction.

This capacity to see systems rather than items marks the maturity of export control practice. It also raises stakes. With greater visibility comes greater responsibility. Decisions informed by data can be precise, but they can also entrench assumptions and blind spots. The map is never the territory.

As export controls grew more sophisticated, so did criticism. Industries complained of uncertainty. Humanitarian groups warned of harm. Some factories shut down not because their products were banned, but because compliance costs became prohibitive. Entire regions felt the chill of controls aimed elsewhere.

In response, a new cohort of reformers emerged. Often trained as engineers or scientists, they brought domain knowledge into policy debates. One such adviser, after witnessing a production line idle because of misclassified components, pushed to redesign control categories. The aim was not to weaken controls but to align them with technical reality. Precision, she argued, could sharpen pressure while sparing civilians.

This tension between security and harm runs through the chapter. Export controls promise selectivity. In practice, they can sprawl. The difference lies in design and review. Where control strategies are updated and informed by feedback, they adapt. Where they ossify, they punish indiscriminately.

The continuity with earlier chapters is deliberate. Like financial sanctions, export controls have become systems rather than events. They rely on professionals interpreting rules under uncertainty. They generate unintended effects through fear and caution. They create architects whose influence exceeds their titles.

Yet export controls differ in one crucial respect. They are closer to material reality. A blocked payment is abstract; a halted shipment is tangible. Containers pile up. Machines sit idle. Patients wait. The consequences are visible to those involved, even if they escape public attention.

This visibility creates its own pressures. Licensing officers know that delay has cost. They also know that error can be catastrophic. The balance is personal. Some officers harden. Others agonise. Institutions offer checklists and escalation paths, but the final judgement often rests with an individual signing a form.

The chapter moves through these layers deliberately. It begins with the evolution from lists to strategies, tracing how control logic became more elastic and more powerful. It then enters the daily work of case officers, where abstract policy meets human need. It expands outward to the engineering of supply-chain visibility, showing how data reshapes enforcement. Finally, it turns to reformers pushing for smarter controls, grounded in technical understanding and ethical concern.

The motif threading these stories is concealment and revelation. Cargo can be hidden in plain sight. Control can be exerted quietly. Decisions that seem minor can redirect flows across continents. Export controls operate by revealing some pathways and closing others, often without public acknowledgement.

Why does this matter now? Because technological diffusion is accelerating, and with it the challenge of controlling use without stifling benefit. Artificial intelligence, advanced manufacturing, and biotechnology blur lines faster than any schedule can keep up. Export controls will only grow in importance. How they are designed will shape not just security outcomes, but economic and humanitarian ones.

This chapter does not argue for more or fewer controls. It argues for seeing them clearly. To understand modern sanctions, one must understand how hidden cargo is traced, how lists give way to judgement, and how ordinary officials decide what moves and what does not. The container in Rotterdam remains unopened as the officer weighs her choice. Somewhere else, a factory waits. Somewhere else, a patient does. The story unfolds in that space between law and life.

From goods lists to control strategies

In October 2013, in Whitehall, a civil servant opened a file marked *post-incident review*. The incident had occurred months earlier, when specialised valves manufactured in the United Kingdom were discovered at a Syrian chemical weapons facility. The valves were not on any prohibited list when exported. The paperwork was clean. The law had been followed. The headlines were unforgiving. Parliament demanded answers. How, with one of the world's most elaborate export control regimes, had this happened?

Lists had failed.

For decades, export controls rested on an assumption that danger could be enumerated. If sensitive goods were named, numbered, and categorised, their movement could be managed. Control schedules grew thicker, more detailed, more technical. They also grew brittle. Technology moved faster than amendments. Dual-use items proliferated. The scandal in Syria did not expose a loophole; it exposed a premise.

This is the hinge.

The thesis that follows is precise. Modern export controls no longer operate primarily through static lists of goods, but through control strategies that embed judgement, intent, and context into licensing practice. This shift did not require new statutes or dramatic announcements. It occurred through changes in definitions, guidance, and logic—quiet architectural moves that altered pressure without altering law.

The civil servant in Whitehall was tasked with redesigning a dual-use licensing scheme that had been technically compliant and strategically ineffective. Her brief was not to tighten the law, but to ensure it could no longer be satisfied by formalism alone. The challenge was conceptual. How could control move from objects to systems without becoming arbitrary?

Observe the first move. Rather than expanding the list, she reinterpreted "knowledge" of end-use. Previously, exporters were required to know, or have reason to believe, that goods would be used for prohibited purposes. The guidance treated this narrowly. After the review, it was broadened. Patterns of procurement, intermediaries, and past behaviour became relevant. Name the shift: contextualisation. Explain that control migrated from item identity to usage environment. The consequence was immediate. Licences that once sailed through were paused.

This change altered behaviour without changing law. Exporters adjusted compliance programmes. Due diligence deepened. Transactions slowed. Pressure increased, invisibly.

Goods lists had always struggled with dual-use reality. A centrifuge component might be innocuous in one factory and dangerous in another. Lists respond by proliferating thresholds: size, tolerance, performance. These technical markers age quickly. Strategies, by contrast, age slower. They ask *why* and *where*, not only *what.*

A second example underscores the point. In 2018, the United States Department of Commerce revised its approach to emerging technologies, signalling that certain artificial intelligence applications could fall under export control even if not yet itemised. The Export Control Reform Act provided authority, but the immediate effect came through guidance. Companies reassessed collaborations. Venture funding shifted. No list had been published. Control was exercised through anticipation.

Name the mechanism: anticipatory compliance. Explain that when strategies are signalled, firms internalise risk before rules crystallise. The consequence is influence without enumeration.

The hinge motif appears again when considering enforcement. Lists invite binary decisions. Strategies invite discretion. Licensing officers became central. Their assessments aggregated into policy. The Whitehall redesign explicitly empowered officers to request additional information, to weigh red flags collectively, and to deny licences on precautionary grounds. Critics warned of subjectivity. Proponents argued necessity.

Metrics reveal the impact. In the year following the redesign, approval rates for certain categories of dual-use exports fell, according to parliamentary testimony in 2015. Export volumes dipped modestly. Diversion incidents declined. The pressure was targeted, but real.

This evolution was not confined to one jurisdiction. The European Union's adoption of "catch-all" controls in the 2000s reflected similar logic, allowing authorities to require licences for items not listed if destined for prohibited use. Catch-all was a strategic concept masquerading as a clause. Its power lay in elasticity.

Yet elasticity carries risk. A credible limitation must be acknowledged. Strategy-based controls can drift into overreach. When definitions expand without clear bounds, uncertainty rises. Small firms struggle. Innovation chills. The danger is not theoretical. After several high-profile denials, industry groups complained of unpredictability. Some investment moved elsewhere. Pressure spread beyond intent.

Reconciling this limitation requires governance. Strategies must be anchored by transparent criteria and review. The Whitehall civil servant insisted on this. Her redesign included internal escalation pathways and periodic reassessment of guidance. Strategy was not meant to replace lists, but to supplement them where lists failed.

Translate abstraction into observable practice. An exporter submits an application for laboratory equipment. Under list logic, the item is uncontrolled. Under strategy logic, the end-user's research focus, funding sources, and procurement history trigger scrutiny. The licence is delayed. The exporter revises contracts. Supply chains adjust. No headline announces the change. The hinge has turned.

The motif surfaces again in language. Terms like "capability" and "potential use" entered guidance. These are not quantifiable like wattage or tensile strength. They require interpretation. Control moved closer to intelligence and further from customs.

The civil servant reflected on the discomfort this caused. Lists allowed her office to say no impersonally. Strategies required explanation. Decisions were challenged. Appeals increased. Yet she argued that accountability improved. Officials could no longer hide behind schedules. They had to articulate reasoning.

This personalisation of control marks the birth of a different administrative ethic. It also reshapes power. Export control authorities, once custodians of lists, became analysts of systems. Their influence grew. So did their burden.

A further example illustrates diffusion. Japan's tightening of export controls on semiconductor materials in 2019 did not add items to a blacklist. It altered licensing procedures, requiring case-by-case review for certain destinations. The effect was immediate. Supply chains faltered. Diplomatic tensions rose. The lever was procedural, not statutory.

The hinge here connected trade to geopolitics without overt sanction. Control strategies allow pressure to be modulated discreetly. They also complicate accountability. When nothing changes on paper, responsibility is harder to assign.

Critics argue that such discretion undermines predictability. Supporters counter that predictability for proliferators is a flaw. Both are right. The trade-off is structural.

The story returns to Whitehall. Months after implementing the redesign, the civil servant reviewed outcomes. There were fewer surprises. There was more friction. Exporters complained, but fewer explanations appeared in parliamentary inquiries. The system felt heavier, but steadier.

The hinge had shifted weight.

The sharpened choice that closes this inquiry is not between lists and strategies, but between denial and discernment. Lists deny with clarity and crudity. Strategies discern with nuance and risk. As technologies converge and uses blur, denial alone will fail. Discernment, poorly governed, will overreach.

Export controls will continue to evolve along this hinge. Those who design them decide how much judgement to embed and how visible to make it. Their choices tighten or relax pressure without fanfare. The valves that once passed unnoticed through customs now turn in offices, guided by definitions that look small and act large.

Case officers on the frontline

On 22 June 2021, in a secure office in Bonn, a licensing officer at Germany's Federal Office for Economic Affairs and Export Control opened a file marked *urgent medical.* The application concerned advanced imaging equipment destined for a hospital in northern Syria. The device could diagnose strokes and tumours with precision unavailable locally. It also contained components capable of high-resolution signal processing, listed as dual-use under EU export control regulations. The end-user certificate was credible. The route was not. The officer checked the clock. Forty-eight hours remained before the hospital's procurement window closed.

The equipment could save lives. It could also be diverted.

Export control regimes are often described as frameworks, strategies, or architectures. None of those words capture where control actually happens. It happens here, at desks like this one, in the hands of case officers charged with translating law into judgement. These officers sit at the fault line between policy intent and human consequence. Their decisions are granular, often solitary, and quietly formative.

The thesis is direct. Case officers are the frontline of export control, exercising discretion that reshapes industries and lives without public acknowledgement. Their work reveals how power in sanctions regimes migrates from statutes to people.

Observe the conditions under which case officers operate. Applications arrive with deadlines and pressure. Legal criteria are clear enough to bind, vague enough to demand interpretation. Intelligence inputs are partial. Commercial arguments are forceful. Humanitarian claims are urgent. Name the role: discretionary gatekeeping. Explain that officers must weigh competing risks without the comfort of certainty. The consequence is that export control becomes personal.

The officer in Bonn began by reviewing the device's technical specifications. Resolution thresholds placed it near, but not beyond, the controlled boundary. The end-user hospital had no known links to prohibited programmes. The transit route passed through a neighbouring country with a mixed compliance record. The law allowed approval with conditions. It also allowed denial on precautionary grounds. Both choices were defensible.

Here the motif emerges: the balance beam. Each decision requires equilibrium between security and need. Lean too far either way and something falls.

Case officers develop instincts over time. They learn which assurances tend to be hollow, which intermediaries obscure rather than clarify, which patterns repeat. These instincts are not codified. They are accumulated. The balance beam narrows with experience.

A second example illustrates scale. In 2019, licensing officers in the United Kingdom faced a surge of applications for machine tools following tightened controls related to China. The tools were standard in automotive manufacturing but adaptable for aerospace use. Approval rates declined modestly. Manufacturers responded by redesigning components to fall below thresholds. Supply chains shifted. The industry adapted to officers' patterns, not to published lists.

Name the phenomenon: regulatory signalling. Explain that case-by-case decisions communicate expectations even without formal guidance. The consequence is that industries reshape themselves around perceived enforcement.

This signalling power is rarely acknowledged. Case officers do not issue press releases. They do not publish rationales. Yet their cumulative decisions set norms. Over time, exporters internalise what will pass and what will stall. Investment follows.

The Bonn officer sought additional information. She requested a detailed installation plan and maintenance agreement tying the equipment to the named hospital. She consulted colleagues in the humanitarian unit. The process slowed. The hospital waited. Patients waited.

The tension is structural. Security risks are diffuse and long-term. Humanitarian needs are immediate and visible. The officer is accountable for the former; she witnesses the latter. The balance beam trembles.

A credible limitation must be acknowledged. Officers are not free agents. Their discretion is bounded by law, policy, and review. Many decisions are straightforward. The argument is not that officers wield unchecked power, but that within their bounds, they shape outcomes profoundly.

Reconciling this limitation requires attention to volume. A single decision seems minor. Thousands form a pattern. The power lies in aggregation.

Metrics illuminate this. According to EU Commission reports from the late 2010s, a small percentage change in approval rates for certain categories correlated with significant trade shifts. The officers did not intend to reshape markets. They did.

The motif returns when decisions are appealed. Appeals consume time and resources. Some officers become more cautious to avoid them. Others grow firmer. Institutional culture matters. In offices where humanitarian considerations are valued, officers lean differently on the beam.

The Bonn officer approved the licence with conditions: on-site verification, restricted servicing, and post-shipment reporting. The equipment shipped. The conditions added cost and delay. The hospital accepted. The patients benefited. The risk was mitigated, not eliminated.

This outcome was neither triumph nor compromise. It was judgement.

Case officers also absorb pressure from multiple directions. Exporters lobby. Ministries signal priorities. Media attention waxes and wanes. Officers are trained to be apolitical, yet their work is inherently political. Every approval and denial participates in foreign policy.

The second echo of the motif appears in fatigue. Over time, constant balancing takes a toll. Officers describe the strain of knowing that error has consequences they may never see. Some harden, preferring denial to doubt. Others seek transfers. Institutions rarely acknowledge this burden.

A further example from Japan underscores the point. After tightening export controls on certain materials in 2019, licensing officers faced intense scrutiny. Approval processes slowed. Companies complained. Diplomats intervened. Officers became lightning rods. The balance beam carried not only security and need, but national pride.

The frontline nature of this work is often invisible to policymakers. Strategies are devised at altitude. Implementation happens at ground level. Feedback is sporadic. Officers adapt silently.

The closing trade-off is unavoidable. Export control regimes can centralise decisions further, reducing discretion but increasing bluntness. Or they can invest in the capacity, training, and support of case officers, acknowledging their role as architects of outcome. Precision lives with people, not paper.

The Bonn officer closed the file late that evening. Another application waited. Somewhere, another balance beam awaited its crossing.

Engineering supply-chain visibility

In May 2019, in an office near the Gare de Lyon in Paris, an analyst at a European customs intelligence unit stared at a heat map that should not have existed. The data showed a sudden surge in exports of specialised ball bearings from a mid-sized manufacturer in northern Italy to a logistics hub in the Caucasus. The bearings were not prohibited. The destination country was not sanctioned. Yet the volumes, when overlaid with shipping logs and corporate registry filings, traced a pattern that ended somewhere else entirely. The analyst circled the anomaly and opened a new file. The diversion was hiding in plain sight.

Supply chains are built to move goods efficiently, not transparently. For decades, export control regimes relied on declarations and trust, reinforced by inspections at the border. That model frays when goods travel through multiple jurisdictions, ownership structures splinter, and components serve multiple ends. The response has been a quiet revolution in visibility. Control has shifted from checkpoints to patterns.

The thesis is exact. Engineering supply-chain visibility has become one of the most powerful tools in modern export control, enabling targeted intervention where blanket bans once seemed the only option. By mapping flows rather than policing items, analysts can expose hidden diversions and offer policymakers precision without paralysis.

Observe the problem that visibility seeks to solve. As controls tightened on certain destinations, trade routes adapted. Goods were re-exported through third countries. Shell companies appeared and vanished. Paper compliance remained immaculate while intent migrated. Name the phenomenon: transhipment laundering. Explain that diversion exploits the fragmentation of oversight across jurisdictions. The consequence is that controls aimed at one node are bypassed by rerouting through another.

The Paris analyst had seen this before, but never with such clarity. She combined three datasets rarely viewed together. Customs export declarations provided volume and destination. Shipping logs revealed routing and transhipment points. Corporate records exposed shared directors and beneficial owners across entities in different countries. Each dataset alone was inconclusive. Together, they formed a map.

The motif here is the overlay. Visibility emerges when layers align.

The bearings in question were suitable for civilian machinery. They were also critical components in precision-guided systems. No list captured the risk. The analyst noticed that the receiving company in the Caucasus shared a director with a trading firm in a Middle Eastern jurisdiction known for lax controls. Shipping manifests showed onward movement within weeks. Payments cleared through a regional bank recently flagged for compliance weaknesses. None of this violated the letter of the law. The pattern violated its spirit.

Name the method: network inference. Explain that by correlating disparate data points, analysts infer relationships that no single record discloses. The consequence is a shift from reactive enforcement to anticipatory control.

This capacity has grown rapidly. Advances in data availability, computing power, and analytical techniques have transformed what was once artisanal intelligence work into semi-systematic practice.

Customs agencies increasingly subscribe to commercial shipping databases. Financial intelligence units share corporate ownership information. Analysts build tools that flag anomalies automatically, then investigate manually.

A second named example illustrates scale. In 2020, analysts at the US Department of Commerce's Bureau of Industry and Security used trade data to identify unusual increases in semiconductor equipment exports to Southeast Asian intermediaries. The goods were controlled for export to China but not to the intermediaries. Subsequent investigation revealed diversion. Rather than banning categories wholesale, authorities added specific entities to the Entity List. Pressure narrowed. Legitimate trade continued elsewhere.

Translate abstraction into behaviour. An exporter files paperwork. A shipment moves. Data records accumulate. An analyst detects a spike. A network graph reveals connections. Policymakers act surgically. The alternative would have been a broad restriction harming unrelated firms.

The overlay motif returns as analysts refine their tools. Each additional dataset sharpens resolution. Satellite imagery confirms warehouse expansion. Insurance records reveal cargo values inconsistent with declared use. Social media traces link executives across firms. Visibility deepens.

Yet this engineering is not neutral. It privileges what can be seen and measured. It can misinterpret coincidence as conspiracy. A credible limitation must be acknowledged. Data-driven visibility risks false inference, particularly in complex markets where trade patterns shift for benign reasons. Overconfidence in maps can lead to overreach.

Reconciling this limitation requires humility and review. The Paris analyst did not act alone. She presented her findings to a multi-agency group, including licensing officers and regional experts. Some anomalies were explained away by seasonal demand. Others persisted. The decision to act rested on convergence, not suspicion.

Metrics matter. According to OECD analysis published in 2019, targeted entity-based controls informed by network analysis reduced evasion attempts more effectively than broad sectoral bans in certain contexts. The evidence was partial but persuasive. Precision paid dividends.

The human element remains central. Data does not interpret itself. Analysts choose thresholds, decide which anomalies merit attention, and frame findings for policymakers. Their judgement shapes outcomes as much as any algorithm.

The motif surfaces again when visibility alters behaviour. Once traders realise that patterns are watched, they adapt. Routes change. Structures grow more complex. Visibility must evolve or stagnate. The map is never complete.

A further example from Japan illustrates adaptation. After analysts exposed a diversion route for advanced materials through a Southeast Asian hub in 2019, exporters rerouted through smaller ports and split consignments. Analysts responded by adjusting models to detect fragmentation. The game continued. Visibility is iterative.

The promise of engineered visibility lies in optionality. Policymakers presented with granular evidence can choose among responses. They can deny specific licences, add named entities, or engage diplomatically with transit states. They are no longer forced to choose between inaction and blanket bans.

This optionality matters for legitimacy. Broad bans are easy to explain but hard to justify when harm is diffuse. Targeted measures grounded in evidence command greater confidence internally, even if they remain opaque externally.

The Paris case concluded quietly. The implicated entities were added to a watchlist. Licences involving the bearings were subjected to enhanced review. The transit country was approached through diplomatic channels. The flow slowed. No announcement was made. The map had done its work.

The overlay motif appears one last time in reflection. Each layer of visibility adds burden. Data must be collected, cleaned, and secured. Privacy concerns arise. Resources are finite. Not every supply chain can be mapped exhaustively.

The sharpened trade-off is clear. Authorities can invest in engineered visibility to apply pressure with discrimination, accepting complexity and uncertainty. Or they can retreat to blunt tools that require less analysis but impose greater harm. As supply chains grow more intricate, the former becomes harder but more necessary.

Engineering visibility does not abolish evasion. It changes its cost. It shifts export control from lists to learning, from prohibition to pattern. In that shift lies the possibility of pressure that is both effective and restrained, provided those reading the maps remember that lines represent lives as well as routes.

Pushing for smarter targeted controls

In November 2017, on the outskirts of Brno in the Czech Republic, a factory producing precision machine components shut its doors for three weeks. The workers were sent home. Orders were cancelled. The cause was not a loss of demand but a licensing delay. A revised export control interpretation had swept a broad category of computer-numerical control subcomponents into a higher risk bracket, even though the parts in question could not meet the tolerances required for any military application. The factory's chief engineer, who had designed the components himself, travelled to Prague to explain this. The law did not disagree with him. The categories did.

The paradox was hard to miss. Controls intended to constrain weapons capability were disabling equipment that could never support it. Pressure was being applied, but to the wrong surface.

From this dissonance emerged a quiet reform movement within export control regimes, led not by diplomats or lawyers but by engineers, physicists, and systems designers who understood the material reality behind regulatory language. Their argument was not that controls should be weaker, but that they should be sharper. The thesis is precise. Export controls become both more effective and less harmful when they are designed with domain knowledge that distinguishes capability from appearance, risk from resemblance.

The engineer who left Brno for Prague did not set out to become a policy adviser. She had spent two decades designing industrial machinery and took pride in understanding tolerances, failure modes, and constraints. When her factory shut down, she traced the cause to a definitional change that treated a broad class of components as potentially strategic. The definition ignored physics. It captured too much.

Observe the sequence. A category is widened to prevent evasion. Name the effect: defensive broadening. Explain that regulators expand definitions to close loopholes, often without granular technical differentiation. The consequence is over-inclusion, where low-risk items are captured alongside high-risk ones.

The engineer argued that the category conflated components capable of sustaining extreme rotational accuracy with those that could not. The distinction mattered. Only the former could be repurposed for advanced weapons systems. She produced test data, schematics, and failure analyses. She spoke in microns, not mandates.

This language was unfamiliar to many in the room. Export control debates often revolve around intent and destination rather than performance thresholds grounded in engineering reality. Her intervention shifted the discussion. Officials realised that the category's breadth was unnecessary. The pressure could be reapplied elsewhere.

Name the intervention: capability calibration. Explain that controls aligned with actual functional thresholds reduce collateral harm while preserving leverage. The consequence was revision without repeal. Guidance was amended. The factory reopened.

This was not an isolated episode. Similar dynamics surfaced in other jurisdictions as controls expanded to cover advanced manufacturing, artificial intelligence, and biotechnology. In October 2022, when the United States introduced sweeping export controls on advanced semiconductor manufacturing equipment destined for China, industry experts warned that the performance thresholds chosen risked capturing equipment incapable of producing cutting-edge chips. Subsequent clarifications narrowed scope. Domain knowledge mattered.

The motif that binds these efforts is sharpening. Blunt tools harm widely; sharpened ones cut precisely.

Reformers advocating smarter controls face structural resistance. Bureaucracies favour simplicity. Broad categories are easier to administer. Precision demands effort, expertise, and constant updating. Yet the cost of imprecision is increasingly visible.

A second named example illustrates scale. In 2019, after Japan tightened export controls on materials critical to semiconductor manufacturing, several downstream industries experienced disruption. Analysts later noted that some materials subject to heightened scrutiny were not suitable for sensitive applications without extensive modification. Engineers involved in policy review argued for tiered controls based on purity and performance. Adjustments followed. Trade stabilised. Pressure remained.

Translate abstraction into behaviour. A regulator revises guidance to include performance benchmarks. Licensing officers receive clearer criteria. Exporters know where they stand. Investment resumes. Security is not compromised. It is clarified.

The credible limitation must be addressed. Domain experts can underestimate misuse risk or overstate benignity. Engineers see what a component cannot do; adversaries may see how to combine it with others. Overconfidence in technical boundaries can create gaps.

Reconciling this limitation requires hybrid judgement. Technical insight must be integrated with intelligence and strategic assessment. The reformers described here did not seek veto power. They sought voice. Controls designed in isolation from material reality fail differently than those designed with it.

The engineer from Brno joined a policy unit as an adviser. Her role was to translate between worlds. She learned to frame arguments not as pleas for exemption but as proposals for efficiency. Narrowing categories, she argued, would free resources to focus on genuine threats. Metrics supported her case. Licence processing times dropped. Appeals declined. Enforcement actions became more targeted.

The motif sharpens again when considering civilian harm. Broad controls often shutter factories, delay medical equipment, and chill research collaboration. These effects are not always visible to policymakers. Engineers bring visibility through specificity. They can point to a production line and say, with evidence, that it cannot serve a prohibited end.

A further example comes from the medical sector. In the late 2010s, export controls affecting advanced imaging components caused delays in equipment delivery to hospitals in sanctioned regions. Biomedical engineers worked with regulators to distinguish diagnostic modules from those adaptable for prohibited research. Revised guidance allowed life-saving equipment to move while retaining scrutiny of higher-risk items. The pressure shifted, not softened.

Metrics again matter. According to industry submissions reviewed by European authorities in 2020, targeted revisions reduced processing delays for low-risk medical exports by weeks without increasing diversion incidents. The data was imperfect but persuasive.

The resistance to such reform often rests on fear. Precision, critics argue, creates loopholes. Broadness feels safer. Yet safety achieved by indiscriminate harm is illusory. It breeds evasion and resentment. Smarter controls seek to concentrate risk rather than diffuse it.

The motif of sharpening appears one last time in institutional culture. Export control regimes that incorporate domain expertise tend to evolve faster. They update categories, consult practitioners, and learn from error. Those that do not ossify. The choice is adaptive sharpness or brittle breadth.

The closing trade-off is operational. Policymakers can continue to widen nets, accepting factory closures and humanitarian spillover as collateral. Or they can invest in expertise that allows nets to be rewoven with intention. This does not eliminate moral hazard. It manages it.

The engineer returned to Brno after her advisory stint. The factory runs again. The controls remain. They are narrower, better aimed. The pressure is where it belongs.

Chapter 4
Hunting Evasion Routes

At 7.18 a.m. on a Tuesday in May 2018, an investigator in a glass tower overlooking Hong Kong harbour refreshed a corporate registry search for the fourth time that week. The company name on her screen had changed again, this time by the addition of a single initial. The address had not. Nor had the nominee director, nor the date of incorporation. On paper, it was a new firm. In practice, it was the same shell wearing a different coat. She added it to a hand-drawn chart pinned beside her desk, where arrows multiplied faster than names. Somewhere inside the tangle lay a sanctioned network that had learned how to disappear without moving.

Sanctions are often described as barriers. Evasion turns them into games of hide-and-seek.

The power of modern sanctions rests on their ability to constrict systems. Their fragility rests on the ingenuity of those who learn to route around them. This chapter enters the space where pressure meets adaptation, where every restriction invites a workaround, and where enforcement becomes less an act of closure than a practice of pursuit. It follows the people whose work is defined not by declarations but by detection: investigators, analysts, and data specialists tasked with finding what was designed not to be found.

Evasion is not an afterthought. It is built into sanctions from the moment they are imposed. When access to markets narrows, incentives to disguise grow. The history of sanctions is therefore inseparable from the history of concealment. What has changed is the scale, speed, and sophistication of the chase. Shell companies can be incorporated in hours. Trade can be rerouted across multiple jurisdictions in weeks. Funds can move through digital channels in seconds. The hunt has become continuous.

This chapter begins with the most familiar tactic: the shell company. Brass-plate firms, cut-outs, and nominee directors have long been tools of illicit finance. What is new is their industrialisation. Corporate service providers now offer off-the-shelf anonymity across jurisdictions. Registers exist, but they rarely connect. Investigators work across languages, time zones, and legal systems, stitching together fragments that were never meant to align.

The Hong Kong investigator's chart grew because she refused to treat each company as a discrete entity. She looked instead for repetition. Same address. Same incorporation agent. Same pattern of activity. Persistence mattered more than revelation. Pattern recognition became the craft. When the network finally emerged, it was less a spider's web than a shadow cast repeatedly in different directions.

From corporate veils, the chapter moves outward to trade routes. Sanctioned goods rarely travel directly once controls tighten. They detour. Third countries become conduits, hubs, or buffers. A customs specialist notices that exports of a niche industrial component to a small state have tripled in six months. The component has no obvious domestic use there. Shipping data confirms onward movement. What appears as trade growth is, on closer inspection, an evasion corridor.

These corridors are not accidental. They are constructed in response to enforcement pressure. When one route closes, another opens. The work of tracking them demands attention to anomalies rather than totals, to spikes rather than averages. It rewards those who ask why something *increased*, not only why it stopped.

The chapter then turns to money, increasingly detached from physical trade. Digital assets, alternative payment platforms, and informal networks offer new ways to move value beyond traditional chokepoints. A small enforcement team develops heuristics to identify sanction evasion in cryptocurrency flows, watching for behavioural patterns rather than addresses alone. The promise is speed and scale. The limitation is adaptation. What can be detected today can be disguised tomorrow.

Across these domains runs a single logic: sanctions enforcement is not a project with an endpoint. It is a contest. Each move by authorities reshapes the field on which the next move is played. A veteran investigator keeps a notebook of familiar tricks—recycled directors, mirrored addresses, shell companies dissolved and reborn. He does not believe in final victories. He believes in staying attentive.

This chapter situates that attentiveness within the broader architecture described earlier in the book. Financial chokepoints and export controls create pressure. Evasion routes relieve it selectively. The interaction between the two determines whether sanctions bite, blur, or backfire. Understanding sanctions, therefore, requires understanding the hunt: who conducts it, how they think, and what they learn about the limits of power.

The stories that follow are not tales of triumph. They are studies in asymmetry. Evasion requires only one open path. Enforcement must watch them all. Yet enforcement possesses its own advantages: time, memory, and accumulation. Patterns that evade detection once often fail the second time. The hunters remember.

The modern relevance is acute. As sanctions expand in scope and ambition, so too does the incentive to circumvent them. Globalisation has not ended; it has fragmented. Supply chains stretch across more jurisdictions, financial flows cross more platforms, and corporate identities multiply. The hunting ground is larger, noisier, and more data-rich than ever before.

This chapter does not promise a master key to evasion. It offers something more durable: an understanding of how concealment works and why it persists. It shows how shell companies are unpicked not by single revelations but by sustained attention, how trade corridors are revealed by anomalies rather than admissions, how digital money both exposes and obscures, and why enforcement remains an unfinished practice.

The hunt continues because the stakes endure. Pressure without pursuit dissipates. Pursuit without understanding misfires. The pages ahead follow those who live in that tension, tracing the routes that sanctions are meant to close and the ingenuity that keeps them open—until it does not.

Chasing shell companies and cut-outs

In September 2017, on the twenty-third floor of an office tower in Central, Hong Kong, an investigator working for a multinational bank noticed that three newly incorporated companies shared the same floor number, the same company secretary, and incorporation dates spaced exactly fourteen days apart. Each firm claimed to trade in unrelated goods. Each had opened an account within hours of incorporation. Each had received funds from a jurisdiction subject to heavy sanctions scrutiny. The addresses were legal. The paperwork was flawless. The pattern was not.

What could not be seen mattered more than what could.

Shell companies are as old as commerce itself, but their role in modern sanctions evasion has changed in character and scale. They are no longer occasional disguises; they are modular components of evasion architectures, assembled, discarded, and reassembled as pressure shifts. The thesis is clear. Sanctions evasion through shell companies is exposed not by revelation or confession, but by sustained pattern recognition carried out by investigators who understand that invisibility leaves traces.

Observe the contemporary shell company. It is cheap, fast, and disposable. In major financial centres, incorporation can take less than a day. Nominee directors and shareholders are supplied as a service. Addresses are recycled. The entity exists to transact briefly and vanish. Name the strategy: transactional anonymity. Explain that shells reduce personal exposure by absorbing risk at the corporate level. The consequence is that enforcement efforts face a moving target with no fixed centre.

The Hong Kong investigator had seen such targets before. She knew better than to treat any single company as decisive. Instead, she mapped connections. Same incorporator. Same bank branch. Same rhythm of transactions. The motif here is the echo. Each shell repeated fragments of another. Individually meaningless, collectively revealing.

Her work followed a rhythm familiar to sanctions professionals. Start with a flagged transaction. Trace ownership. Hit a dead end. Go sideways. Look for repetition rather than explanation. Persistence replaced intuition. Over weeks, she built a visual map on a whiteboard, arrows crossing names that never appeared together in filings. The network slowly cohered.

A second example from London illustrates the method's portability. In 2015, investigators at the UK's National Crime Agency dismantled a network of shell companies used to move funds linked to sanctioned entities through the City. The firms were incorporated years apart, under different names, and operated in different sectors. What bound them was mundane: identical misspellings in incorporation documents and a shared postal code. The pattern had survived change.

Name the craft: forensic monotony. Explain that evasion relies on repetition because creating perfect novelty is costly. The consequence is that networks betray themselves through the very efficiencies that make them viable.

Shell companies rarely operate alone. They are cut-outs—buffers between principals and transactions. They hold accounts, sign contracts, and dissolve. The principals remain unseen. Investigators learn to treat shells not as actors but as instruments.

This perspective shifts the hunt. Rather than asking *who owns this company*, investigators ask *why does this company exist*. They examine transaction lifespans, revenue diversity, and operational depth. A firm with no employees, minimal overhead, and high transaction velocity invites scrutiny. Metrics replace motives.

The Hong Kong case advanced when the investigator overlaid timing. Each shell received funds shortly after incorporation, moved them through correspondent accounts within days, and went dormant. The cycle repeated with a new name. This cadence was more informative than ownership.

Yet the work is slow. Each step requires legal caution. Banks cannot assume guilt. Regulators demand evidence. Networks exploit this friction. By the time one shell is understood, another has replaced it.

A credible limitation must be faced. Shell companies are not inherently illicit. They are used legitimately for tax planning, joint ventures, and risk isolation. Overzealous pattern detection risks false positives, chilling lawful activity. Reconciling this limitation requires corroboration. Patterns must align across multiple dimensions—timing, counterparties, behaviour—not merely appearance.

The Hong Kong investigator did not act alone. She coordinated with colleagues in Singapore and Frankfurt, sharing anonymised indicators. Similar patterns emerged. The echo widened. When law enforcement became involved, the case rested not on a single smoking gun but on convergence. The network could not explain its repetition.

The motif returns when the network adapts. After accounts were frozen, incorporations shifted to a neighbouring jurisdiction. Directors changed. Addresses moved. The echo softened but did not disappear. Investigators adjusted their lens, looking for subtler repetitions. The chase continued.

This cat-and-mouse dynamic reveals a deeper truth. Shell companies succeed not because they are invisible, but because attention is scarce. They rely on fragmentation: each jurisdiction sees a fragment, each institution sees a slice. Investigators who bridge silos gain advantage.

Technology aids this bridging, but it does not replace judgement. Databases can surface similarities, but humans decide which matter. The Hong Kong investigator's whiteboard was not redundant. It externalised memory. It allowed intuition to meet evidence.

Metrics again matter. According to a 2018 FATF report, complex corporate structures remain among the most common vehicles for sanctions evasion and money laundering. The report emphasised pattern analysis over ownership disclosure alone. Transparency without synthesis is insufficient.

The human cost of failure is often abstracted. Shell companies move money that funds procurement, weapons, or repression. Yet the immediate harm of enforcement missteps can fall on innocents. Accounts frozen by mistake disrupt livelihoods. Investigators carry this weight quietly.

The echo motif surfaces one final time in resolution. When the Hong Kong network was finally designated, dozens of shell companies were named. Most had already dissolved. The principals were identified through separate means. The shells had done their work and vanished. Yet the map remained. Future cases moved faster.

The sharpened choice at the close is methodological. Enforcement can continue to chase shells individually, reacting to names and addresses. Or it can invest in pattern literacy—training investigators to see repetition, rhythm, and absence as evidence. The former will always lag. The latter compresses the gap.

Shell companies promise invisibility. They deliver only delay. For those patient enough to listen for echoes, the network eventually speaks.

Tracking trade through third countries

In April 2020, in a customs analysis unit overlooking the Bosphorus, a Turkish trade specialist noticed an anomaly that did not fit the season. Exports of a niche industrial adhesive to a small Central Asian state had tripled in six months. The adhesive was used primarily in aerospace manufacturing. The destination country had no such industry. The paperwork was impeccable. The trade statistics were public. The surge made no sense.

Trade rarely lies. Patterns do.

Sanctions regimes are designed to block direct exchange between designated actors and global markets. Their effectiveness therefore depends on what happens when trade takes the long way round. Third countries—neither sanctioned nor neutral bystanders—become conduits, buffers, and sometimes beneficiaries of rerouted commerce. The thesis here is clear. The most consequential sanctions evasion does not hide; it detours. Those who trace trade through third countries expose evasion corridors by treating anomalies as signals rather than noise.

Observe the structural incentive. When direct exports are prohibited, firms and intermediaries seek jurisdictions with permissive oversight, strategic geography, or plausible demand. Goods flow legally to these hubs, then onward informally or through re-export. Name the tactic: triangulation. Explain that triangulation fragments responsibility across borders, diluting accountability. The consequence is that enforcement must reconstruct intent across jurisdictions that see only pieces.

The Turkish specialist began with questions rather than accusations. Why this product? Why now? Why here? She pulled historical data. The adhesive had never exceeded modest volumes. She overlaid shipping records. Containers moved onward within weeks, often to ports near sanctioned destinations. Payment records, shared under bilateral arrangements, showed settlement through a regional bank recently flagged for compliance weaknesses. Each piece alone was ambiguous. Together, they suggested a corridor.

The motif here is the bend. Trade bends around obstacles. The curve reveals pressure.

Her work illustrates a broader shift in sanctions enforcement. Analysts increasingly focus on rate-of-change rather than absolute volume. A sudden spike in exports to an unlikely market is more informative than a steady stream to a known one. This sensitivity to deviation distinguishes detection from bookkeeping.

A second named example reinforces the method. In 2017, South Korean customs officials detected unusual increases in refined petroleum product exports to Singapore following tightened sanctions on North Korea. Singapore's domestic consumption did not explain the volumes. Subsequent investigation revealed ship-to-ship transfers at sea, with fuel diverted onward. The detection hinged on comparative analysis, not tip-offs. The bend was visible in the data.

Name the practice: anomaly-led investigation. Explain that analysts treat unexpected changes as entry points for inquiry. The consequence is proactive enforcement that adapts as evasion adapts.

The Turkish specialist mapped the corridor further. She examined corporate registries of the importing firms. Many were newly established, with minimal staff and shared directors. Shipping manifests revealed consistent use of the same freight forwarders. Insurance records showed elevated premiums inconsistent with benign trade. The corridor thickened.

Third countries are rarely passive in these arrangements. Some benefit economically from acting as hubs. Others lack capacity to monitor re-exports effectively. Diplomatic sensitivity complicates response. Accusing a partner state of facilitating evasion carries cost.

Translate abstraction into behaviour. A customs analyst drafts a report. Supervisors weigh evidence. Diplomatic channels are engaged quietly. Exporters are warned. Licences are scrutinised. Trade slows. No public sanction is announced. Pressure is applied indirectly.

The motif bends again when routes shift. After scrutiny increased, adhesive exports dipped. Within months, a different component—less obviously linked to aerospace—spiked. The corridor adjusted. The bend moved.

A credible limitation must be acknowledged. Not every anomaly signals evasion. Trade patterns can change for benign reasons: new infrastructure, temporary demand, supply chain disruptions. Overinterpreting data risks false accusations and strained relations. Reconciling this limitation requires patience and corroboration.

The Turkish specialist waited. She compared similar products. She consulted industry experts. She tracked downstream movements.

Only when multiple indicators aligned did she escalate. Precision mattered.

Metrics support the approach. According to a 2019 World Customs Organization report, targeted investigations triggered by trade anomalies led to higher interdiction rates than random inspections in several pilot jurisdictions. The evidence was not uniform, but the trend was clear. Watching the bends worked.

The human dimension of this work is often overlooked. Analysts spend hours with spreadsheets and maps, developing an intuition for normality. When normal shifts, they feel it. This tacit knowledge resists automation. Algorithms can flag spikes. Humans decide which matter.

The corridor motif appears again in geopolitics. Some states find themselves repeatedly used as transit hubs. Their officials bristle at implication. Cooperation improves when presented with evidence rather than accusation. Data becomes a diplomatic tool.

A further example from the Baltic region illustrates cooperation. After analysts detected unusual exports of specialised machinery to a small Caucasus state in 2018, authorities shared findings bilaterally. The transit state tightened oversight. The corridor narrowed. Trade normalised. Pressure was applied without rupture.

The limits of corridor tracking are real. Evasion routes can fragment into micro-flows below detection thresholds. Goods can be disassembled. Services can substitute for products. Analysts chase moving curves.

Yet the value remains. Corridor analysis reframes sanctions enforcement as spatial reasoning. It asks not only *who* and *what*, but *how* and *where*. It accepts that evasion is adaptive and seeks to follow adaptation.

The bend motif returns one final time in reflection. Trade bends where pressure is uneven. Where controls tighten abruptly, curves appear. Where enforcement learns, curves flatten. The process is iterative.

The sharpened trade-off at the close is strategic. Authorities can treat third-country trade as external to sanctions design, reacting only when violations surface. Or they can integrate anomaly detection into ongoing review, recognising that evasion routes are part of the system, not exceptions to it. The latter demands attention and restraint. It also yields options short of escalation.

The Turkish specialist filed her final report in late summer. The adhesive exports stabilised. A different anomaly would soon appear elsewhere. She would watch for the bend.

Following money in digital form

On 21 August 2021, in a windowless room inside a regulatory building in Washington, DC, a three-person analytics team watched a cluster of cryptocurrency addresses light up on a shared screen. The pattern had appeared before. Funds moved in short bursts, paused, then fanned out through dozens of wallets before reconverging at an exchange registered in Eastern Europe. The total value was modest by market standards. The timing was not. The flows coincided with a new sanctions designation announced that morning. The team tagged the cluster and began annotating behaviour. Five screens. No noise.

Digital money leaves footprints.

For a decade, cryptocurrencies were framed as a sanctions escape hatch: borderless, pseudonymous, and resistant to control. That framing was always incomplete. Public blockchains record every transaction, forever. What they conceal is identity, not movement. The thesis here is exact. Digital assets have transformed sanctions enforcement not by erasing traces, but by shifting the hunt from institutions to patterns, creating new opportunities for detection alongside new limits.

Observe the early assumption. Because cryptocurrencies do not rely on correspondent banks, it was assumed they would evade chokepoints. Name the belief: infrastructural bypass. Explain that evasion was expected to follow the path of least regulated rails. The consequence was anxiety, sometimes exaggerated, about sanctions collapse.

Reality intervened. Blockchain analytics matured. Enforcement learned to read flows rather than names. The Washington team belonged to a unit that combined financial intelligence with data science. They did not chase individual wallets. They built heuristics.

The motif binding their work is the trace. Not a line, but a residue. Each transaction leaves a residue of timing, counterparties, and structure. The trace persists even as addresses change.

The team's first heuristic focused on rhythm. Sanctions evasion often requires speed after designation. Funds move quickly to avoid freezing. Clusters that spiked immediately after announcements drew attention. The second heuristic examined fragmentation. Legitimate users consolidated for efficiency; evaders fragmented to obscure. The third looked at reconvergence. Money scattered rarely stayed scattered.

Name the method: behavioural clustering. Explain that by grouping transactions by behaviour rather than ownership, analysts infer coordination. The consequence is that anonymity weakens.

A named example illustrates impact. In September 2021, the US Treasury's Office of Foreign Assets Control designated Suex, a cryptocurrency exchange accused of facilitating ransomware payments. The designation relied heavily on blockchain analysis showing consistent interaction with illicit clusters. Exchanges worldwide adjusted controls. Flows shifted. The trace had guided action.

The Washington team refined its tools. They overlaid blockchain data with off-chain information: exchange compliance reports, IP metadata shared under legal process, and typologies from the

Financial Action Task Force. Each layer improved confidence. None was decisive alone.

The trace motif reappears when limits surface. Privacy-enhancing technologies, such as mixers and privacy coins, deliberately blur traces. Analysts adapt by examining entry and exit points. Mixers obscure paths internally but still connect to the wider network. Traces bend, they do not vanish.

A second named example underscores the point. In 2022, after sanctions on Russia intensified following the invasion of Ukraine, analysts monitored increased use of certain decentralised exchanges. Volumes rose. So did scrutiny. According to Chainalysis's 2022 report, sanctioned entities' use of cryptocurrency grew in absolute terms but remained a small fraction of global volume. The fear of wholesale bypass did not materialise. The trace constrained scale.

Translate abstraction into behaviour. An entity receives funds. It routes them through a mixer. It exits at an exchange. The exchange applies know-your-customer checks. Funds freeze. The path was obscured, but the exit was visible.

The Washington team learned to be cautious. Not every suspicious pattern indicated sanctions evasion. Traders arbitrage volatility. Privacy advocates use mixers for benign reasons. Overreach risks chilling legitimate activity and undermining trust. Reconciling this limitation required thresholds and review.

Name the constraint: probabilistic enforcement. Explain that blockchain analysis produces likelihoods, not certainties. The consequence is that enforcement must accept ambiguity.

The team instituted internal review boards. Flags required corroboration. Behavioural signals had to align with contextual factors, such as timing around sanctions announcements or links to known networks. This slowed action. It improved accuracy.

The motif returns as time. Digital flows move fast. Review takes longer. The gap matters. Evaders exploit delay. Enforcement balances speed against error.

A further example from Europe highlights coordination. In 2023, several European regulators collaborated with exchanges to develop real-time alerts for high-risk clusters. The initiative reduced lag but raised privacy concerns. Civil society groups questioned scope. The trade-off sharpened.

Digital assets also expose institutional seams. Sanctions regimes are national; blockchains are global. Jurisdictional gaps persist. An exchange compliant in one country may be permissive in another. Funds route accordingly. Analysts map not only flows, but regulatory gradients.

Name the practice: jurisdictional arbitrage detection. Explain that evaders exploit uneven oversight. The consequence is that enforcement effectiveness depends on international alignment.

The Washington team's work fed into diplomacy. Evidence of routing through certain platforms informed discussions with foreign regulators. Some tightened rules. Others demurred. The trace influenced policy indirectly.

The promise of data-driven enforcement is scale. Algorithms can monitor millions of transactions. The limit is interpretation. Machines flag; humans decide. The team resisted full automation. They had seen false patterns mislead before.

The motif of trace surfaces again in memory. Blockchains remember. Investigations can look backward indefinitely. A transaction unnoticed today may matter tomorrow. This persistence alters incentives. Evaders cannot rely on forgetting.

Yet persistence cuts both ways. Mistakes persist too. Incorrect attribution can haunt addresses and users. Governance matters.

The sharpened trade-off at the close is strategic. Authorities can treat digital assets as an exceptional threat, responding with broad restrictions that risk pushing activity underground. Or they can invest in behavioural analysis, accepting nuance and uncertainty to apply pressure where it counts. The latter demands patience and restraint.

On the Washington screen, the cluster faded as funds dispersed. Notes remained. The trace was recorded. Another designation would come. Another pattern would appear. Digital money runs fast. Memory runs longer.

The cat-and-mouse of enforcement

In February 2014, in a modest office near The Hague, a veteran sanctions investigator opened a battered notebook and wrote the same three words he had written dozens of times before: *same actor again*. The case involved a shipping intermediary recently flagged for facilitating trade with Iran. The name was new. The phone number was not. Nor was the freight forwarder. Nor was the pattern of invoices arriving just below reporting thresholds. The investigator paused, drew a small circle beside the entry, and turned the page. He had seen this before.

Sanctions move. Evasion moves faster.

From the outside, sanctions enforcement is often imagined as linear: rules are written, violations detected, penalties imposed. From the inside, it looks recursive. Every control creates incentives to adapt. Every enforcement action teaches lessons to those watching. The thesis here is blunt. Sanctions enforcement is not a campaign with an endpoint, but an ongoing contest shaped by learning on both sides, where advantage accrues to those who remember.

The investigator's notebook was not nostalgia. It was method. He kept it because systems forget. Staff rotate. Databases update. Patterns repeat under new guises. The notebook preserved institutional memory in a form that survived restructuring and software migrations. It recorded tricks, aliases, and behaviours that resurfaced years later. The motif that binds this chapter is the loop. Enforcement advances in loops, not lines.

Observe the basic dynamic. A sanctions measure closes a channel. Evaders probe for alternatives. When an alternative proves viable, it spreads. Enforcement detects the spread and responds. Name the process: adaptive cycling. Explain that each side iterates based on feedback from the other. The consequence is that no control remains effective indefinitely without adjustment.

The 2014 case illustrates this cycle. After correspondent banking restrictions tightened on Iranian trade, intermediaries shifted to third-country routing. When that drew scrutiny, they fragmented shipments. When fragmentation raised flags, they diversified commodities. Each adaptation exploited a lag between control and response.

The investigator recognised the lag as the critical variable. Enforcement is deliberative by design. It requires evidence, legal review, and coordination. Evasion exploits speed and dispersion. The contest is asymmetric.

A second named example underscores the point. Following the 2012 SWIFT disconnection of Iranian banks, traders turned to informal payment mechanisms and barter arrangements. Oil-for-goods deals proliferated. Enforcement responded by targeting facilitators and insurers. Traders adapted again, using layered shell companies and reinsurance. The loop tightened.

Name the insight: path dependence. Explain that early enforcement choices shape the forms evasion later takes. The consequence is that mistakes echo.

The investigator's notebook captured these echoes. A recycled actor might disappear for years, then reappear in a different sector. The same freight forwarder turned up in a proliferation case after appearing in a sanctions evasion matter a decade earlier. Memory linked them.

This memory is unevenly distributed. Institutions lose it through turnover. Evaders retain it through continuity of networks. The notebook was an attempt to rebalance.

The loop motif returns when enforcement succeeds. A designation disrupts a network. Assets freeze. Public attention spikes. For a time, activity drops. Then, slowly, fragments recombine elsewhere. Success plants the seeds of the next round.

A credible limitation must be acknowledged. Not all repetition indicates evasion. Some behaviours recur because they are efficient or conventional. Overinterpreting loops risks chasing ghosts. Reconciling this limitation requires discernment. Patterns must persist across contexts to matter.

The investigator relied on corroboration. He compared notes with colleagues in customs, banking, and intelligence. When the same names surfaced independently, confidence grew. The loop closed.

Metrics illustrate the challenge. According to US Treasury assessments in the late 2010s, enforcement actions produced short-term compliance spikes followed by gradual erosion as evasion techniques diffused. The data suggested diminishing returns without adaptation. Learning was essential.

The cat-and-mouse dynamic intensifies with technology. Digital platforms accelerate both enforcement and evasion. Analysts detect patterns faster. Evaders test new tools faster still. The loop compresses.

A further example from cryptocurrency enforcement illustrates compression. After mixers came under scrutiny, evaders shifted to decentralised exchanges. When those exchanges faced compliance pressure, peer-to-peer transfers rose. Enforcement adapted by focusing on entry and exit points. The loop tightened but did not end.

The investigator watched this with weary clarity. Tools changed. Behaviour rhymed. His notebook added new entries, but the old ones stayed relevant. The same tricks resurfaced under different protocols.

This recurrence reveals a deeper constraint. Sanctions enforcement depends on governance structures that change slowly. Evasion networks operate in the gaps between jurisdictions, exploiting uneven oversight. Closing one gap often opens another elsewhere.

Translate abstraction into behaviour. A regulator issues guidance. Banks tighten controls. Traders reroute. Analysts flag anomalies. Policymakers revise rules. The cycle repeats. No step is final.

The loop motif appears again in personnel. Enforcement teams train new staff who rediscover old tricks. Veterans mentor them, passing down heuristics. When veterans retire, some knowledge goes with them. Institutions attempt to codify lessons. Codification lags practice.

The investigator's notebook was his answer to lag. He believed that enforcement lost not because evaders were smarter, but because enforcers forgot. Memory was a weapon.

The human cost of this contest is rarely acknowledged. Enforcement professionals live with uncertainty. They know that today's success is provisional. They rarely see closure. Burnout is common. Yet many stay, driven by the belief that narrowing options matters even if elimination is impossible.

A final example from maritime enforcement captures the ethos. After repeated efforts to curb ship-to-ship transfers of sanctioned oil, authorities tightened monitoring. Vessels adapted by falsifying transponders. Enforcement developed anomaly detection for AIS data. Ships went dark. Satellites filled some gaps. The loop continued.

The sharpened trade-off that closes this inquiry is strategic. Sanctions enforcement can be treated as episodic, responding to crises with bursts of action, then declaring victory. Or it can be treated as a continuous practice that invests in memory, adaptation, and humility. The former breeds complacency. The latter accepts that success is measured in friction imposed, not finality achieved.

The investigator closed his notebook at the end of the day. Another entry waited. He did not expect to finish the hunt. He expected to keep it honest.

Chapter 5
Designing Humanitarian Exceptions

On a dusty afternoon in August 2018, a convoy of aid trucks sat idle at a border crossing in the Middle East. Their cargo was unremarkable and essential: sacks of flour, cartons of antibiotics, water purification tablets. The drivers had permits. The destination hospitals were known. The delay did not come from soldiers or militias, but from a clause. A single phrase in a sanctions exemption—ambiguous, well-intentioned, and untested—had triggered concern at a correspondent bank thousands of miles away. Until clarity arrived, the trucks would not move.

Sanctions had allowed the aid. The system had not.

Humanitarian exceptions are often described as safety valves: narrow openings cut into sanctions regimes to prevent pressure from crushing civilians. In practice, they are among the most fragile elements of modern economic coercion. They depend on legal precision, institutional trust, and human judgement aligning under stress. When any one of these falters, the valve sticks.

This chapter enters that fragile space. It examines how humanitarian carve-outs are designed, negotiated, interpreted, and measured—and why so many fail quietly even when drafted with care. It follows the people who build them: lawyers weighing words against consequences, intermediaries persuading fearful banks, case officers deciding transactions where delay can mean death, and researchers trying to determine whether any of it works.

The need for humanitarian exceptions is not disputed. Sanctions architects have long insisted that pressure should fall on regimes, not populations. Food, medicine, fuel for hospitals, salaries for aid workers—these are almost always excluded on paper. The difficulty lies not in intent but in execution. Exemptions exist within systems designed to prevent risk, not to enable compassion.

The chapter opens with the craft of carve-outs. Drafting an exemption is an exercise in constrained imagination. Too narrow, and legitimate aid is blocked. Too broad, and evasion routes open. A practitioner tasked with designing a licensing scheme for food and medicine after grim field reports learns this quickly. Every adjective matters. Does "medical equipment" include spare parts? Does "humanitarian organisation" require registration in a specific jurisdiction? Each choice shapes behaviour downstream.

These choices are rarely revisited publicly. They appear as footnotes in regulations, yet they decide whether aid flows. The lawyer drafting them understands that her words will be read not by courts but by compliance officers scanning for reasons to say no. Precision is not elegance; it is survival.

From drafting tables, the chapter moves into negotiation rooms. Even the best-designed exemption means little if banks refuse to process the transactions it permits. Here, humanitarian intermediaries step in—individuals fluent in both aid operations and financial risk. They spend days in front of sceptical risk committees, explaining why a particular corridor is lawful, monitored, and necessary. Their task is persuasion under asymmetry: one mistake for the bank could bring penalties; one refusal for the aid agency could stop treatment.

Fear looms large. Enforcement actions have taught banks that intent offers little protection. Over-compliance becomes rational. Humanitarian exceptions hollow out not through prohibition but through caution. The intermediary's success depends less on law than on trust, and trust is scarce when penalties are severe and guidance ambiguous.

The chapter then tightens its focus further, into the offices of case officers handling urgent licence applications. These are not abstractions. A fuel shipment to keep hospital generators running. Salaries for medical staff during a cholera outbreak. Oxygen cylinders during a pandemic surge. The officer reviewing the file knows that delay has consequences measured in hours, not quarters. She also knows that error could expose her institution to sanction.

These decisions are made under time pressure, often with incomplete information. The officer balances verification against urgency, documentation against deterioration. She lives with outcomes she may never see directly. Approval brings relief. Delay brings unease. Denial brings silence.

Across these scenes runs a quiet ethical tension. Sanctions regimes rely on discretion to function, yet humanitarian exceptions ask discretion to bend towards urgency. The same systems that punish speed and reward caution are asked, briefly, to do the opposite. The friction is structural.

The chapter does not stop at design and delivery. It asks a harder question: do humanitarian exceptions actually work? Measuring success is notoriously difficult. Aid flows fluctuate for many reasons. Licences approved do not guarantee goods delivered. Ground reports are partial. A researcher attempting to compare regimes across countries and years finds data that refuses to align. Approvals rise while shortages persist. Shipments increase while clinics still ration.

This difficulty matters. Without measurement, failures are anecdotal and successes assumed. Exemptions become articles of faith rather than tools subject to improvement. The researcher's work suggests that feedback loops are weak where they exist at all. Humanitarian exceptions are drafted, implemented, and rarely revisited.

Throughout the chapter, a motif recurs: the narrow passage. Humanitarian carve-outs create passages through systems designed to block flow. These passages are narrow by design, but they are also easily obstructed by uncertainty, fear, and misalignment. Aid trucks wait at borders. Payments sit pending. Hospitals improvise.

The modern relevance is stark. As sanctions regimes expand in scope and ambition, humanitarian exceptions carry more weight and more strain. Conflicts are protracted. Health systems are fragile. Financial infrastructure is cautious. The margin for error shrinks.

Yet the theme resonates beyond the present moment. It touches an older question about power and restraint. How does a system built to coerce learn to accommodate mercy without undermining itself? How do institutions trained to avoid risk learn to accept it when lives depend on movement?

This chapter does not offer simple answers. It offers portraits of people working inside the tension, making choices that rarely appear in public debates but determine whether principles translate into practice. It shows how a sentence in a regulation can halt a convoy, how a conversation in a boardroom can reopen a corridor, how a signature on a licence can keep lights on in an operating theatre.

The pages that follow trace these efforts without romanticism. They show the limits of goodwill and the costs of fear. They ask whether humanitarian exceptions can be designed not as afterthoughts, but as integral parts of sanctions systems—tested, trusted, and revised.

The trucks at the border eventually moved. The clause was clarified. The delay was measured in days, not weeks. Somewhere else, another convoy waited. The work of designing humanitarian exceptions never ends, because the systems they inhabit are always under pressure.

Crafting carve-outs under pressure

In November 2016, in a cramped office in Brussels, a sanctions lawyer working with the European External Action Service stared at a draft licence text while a radio murmured reports from Aleppo. Hospitals were running out of antibiotics. Fuel stocks were low. The Council had agreed, in principle, that food and medicine must be exempt from the Syria sanctions regime. The problem lay in eight words: *"medical equipment, including related services."* No one could agree what they covered. The lawyer underlined the phrase, circled it, and began again.

Words can stop trucks.

Humanitarian carve-outs are built under pressure that is both moral and procedural. They are drafted at speed, often in response to deteriorating conditions on the ground, and inserted into legal frameworks designed primarily to restrict, not enable. The thesis is straightforward. Humanitarian carve-outs succeed or fail not at the level of intent, but at the level of language, where small drafting choices determine how risk is perceived and whether lawful aid moves at all.

Observe the conditions under which carve-outs are written. Policymakers receive reports from the field: shortages, delays, preventable deaths. Political agreement forms quickly around the need to act. Legal teams are tasked with translating that urgency into text that will withstand scrutiny by banks, insurers, and auditors. Time is short. Consensus is fragile. Every comma carries weight.

Name the craft: defensive drafting. Explain that carve-outs must anticipate not only how aid agencies will read them, but how the most risk-averse institution might. The consequence is that drafters often prioritise certainty over breadth, narrowing exemptions to ensure acceptance. The narrowing can suffocate effect.

The Brussels lawyer understood this tension. She had spent years drafting sanctions measures. This task felt different. The carve-out would not be enforced against violators; it would be tested by those looking for reasons not to act. Banks would scan the text for ambiguity and default to caution. Aid agencies would scan for permission and hope.

Her first instinct was to list goods exhaustively. Flour, rice, antibiotics, vaccines. The list grew. Then she stopped. Lists age quickly. New needs emerge. Spare parts for diagnostic machines are not obviously "medical equipment" until the machine fails. She erased the list and tried a definition instead.

The motif threading this work is the hinge. A carve-out is a hinge in a rigid system, meant to open smoothly under load. If poorly aligned, it jams.

The hinge jammed repeatedly in early sanctions regimes. A second example illustrates the cost. In 2012, after broad sanctions on Iran intensified, humanitarian trade was formally exempt. Yet banks withdrew from processing even licit transactions. According to a 2013 report by Human Rights Watch, shortages of specialised medicines followed, not because they were banned, but because payment channels closed. The exemption existed. The hinge stuck.

Name the phenomenon: permission without pathway. Explain that legal allowance means little without operational routes. The consequence is humanitarian harm despite formal compliance.

The Brussels lawyer revised her approach. She consulted compliance officers informally. What language would give them comfort? They wanted clarity on counterparties, documentation, and monitoring. She added conditions. Aid agencies would need to certify end-use. Transactions would be reported periodically. Oversight reassured banks but burdened delivery.

The hinge creaked.

This is where negotiators enter. Carve-outs are rarely the product of lawyers alone. Diplomats, humanitarian specialists, and sometimes bankers weigh in. Each brings a different fear. Diplomats fear loopholes. Humanitarians fear paralysis. Banks fear penalties.

The Brussels draft circulated. Comments returned overnight. One delegation insisted on narrowing "medical supplies" to items on the World Health Organization's essential medicines list. Another warned that the list excluded paediatric formulations in use locally. A third asked whether fuel for hospital generators counted as humanitarian. Silence followed.

Translate abstraction into behaviour. A lawyer revises text. A negotiator pushes back. An aid agency sends an urgent email. A bank flags uncertainty. Trucks idle.

The hinge motif appears again in field reports. Aid agencies reported that shipments cleared customs but stalled at payment. Banks cited uncertainty over "related services". Did transport count? Insurance? The carve-out was meant to open a door; it had created a corridor with locked side gates.

A credible limitation must be faced. Carve-outs cannot be infinitely permissive. Broad exemptions can be exploited. Goods intended for civilians can be diverted. Fuel can power military vehicles. Reconciling this requires balance, not denial.

The Brussels lawyer acknowledged the risk. She inserted safeguards. End-use verification. Audit rights. These reassured some banks. Others remained unmoved. The fear of enforcement outweighed the promise of clarity.

Metrics from subsequent reviews show the pattern. In several regimes studied by the UN Office for the Coordination of Humanitarian Affairs between 2015 and 2019, the presence of formal exemptions correlated weakly with aid flow. The determining factor was bank participation. Where banks engaged, carve-outs functioned. Where they did not, exemptions remained theoretical.

The lawyer's final draft replaced "including related services" with "and necessary transport, insurance, and ancillary services directly supporting delivery". The language was longer, less elegant, and more explicit. It reduced interpretive space. Banks preferred that.

The hinge moved.

The episode reveals an uncomfortable truth. Humanitarian carve-outs are not drafted for courts; they are drafted for compliance desks. Their audience is not the public, but the most cautious reader in the chain. This shapes language towards operational clarity rather than moral statement.

The motif returns when carve-outs are revisited. Rarely do they receive systematic review. When harm persists, new exemptions are layered on top of old ones, increasing complexity. Hinges multiply. Alignment suffers.

A further example from Yemen illustrates accumulation. Over successive sanctions rounds, exemptions for food, fuel, and medical supplies were added piecemeal. Aid agencies struggled to determine which applied. Banks struggled more. The system became legible only to specialists. Delays persisted.

The Brussels lawyer reflected on this months later. The licence scheme she drafted functioned better than its predecessor. Trucks moved more often. Not always. She resisted calling it success. She called it *less failure.*

The sharpened choice at the close is practical. Policymakers can treat humanitarian carve-outs as symbolic assurances, drafted quickly and left to fend for themselves in risk-averse systems. Or they can treat them as operational instruments, tested against real compliance behaviour and revised accordingly. The former satisfies principle. The latter saves time.

Under pressure, words decide movement. The lawyer knew that the next crisis would demand another hinge. She would open her old drafts, trace where they bent, and adjust again. The work is never finished, because pressure never eases.

Negotiating with sceptical banks

On a rainy morning in March 2019, in a glass-walled conference room overlooking the City of London, a humanitarian finance intermediary waited while a bank's risk committee finished reviewing its agenda. Item seven concerned a proposed payment corridor for medical supplies into Yemen. The amount was modest. The exemption was explicit. The intermediary had provided licences, end-user certificates, audit trails. When the chair finally spoke, it was not about legality. It was about memory. "We were fined in 2014," he said. "Why should we believe this is different?"

Fear travels further than law.

Humanitarian exceptions do not fail at borders alone. They fail in boardrooms where risk is priced, reputations are weighed, and institutional memory is shaped by enforcement actions rather than regulatory text. The thesis is precise. The effectiveness of humanitarian carve-outs depends less on what the law permits than on whether banks believe that permission will protect them when something goes wrong.

Observe the intermediary's role. She is neither aid worker nor banker, but a translator between them. She speaks compliance fluently and humanitarian urgency with equal discipline. Her work begins where exemptions end: at the point where lawful activity must pass through institutions designed to minimise exposure, not maximise benefit.

Name the dynamic: asymmetric risk perception. Explain that for banks, the downside of a single mistake can dwarf the upside of facilitating hundreds of lawful transactions. The consequence is rational over-compliance, even in the face of clear exemptions.

The intermediary knew the committee's history. In 2014, the bank had paid a substantial penalty for sanctions violations unrelated to humanitarian trade. The enforcement action had left scars. Controls tightened. Correspondent relationships shrank. The lesson absorbed was blunt: ambiguity is dangerous, and even compliance offers limited shelter.

She began not with appeals to principle, but with structure. She laid out the corridor: counterparties vetted, transactions capped, reporting automated. She showed how funds would move and where they would stop. She emphasised reversibility. If concerns arose, the corridor could close. The hinge motif returns here. The bank needed assurance that the door could shut quickly.

A second named example underscores the pattern. In 2017, several European banks withdrew entirely from processing humanitarian payments to Somalia despite broad exemptions, citing residual risk. According to a study by the Overseas Development Institute that year, aid agencies faced months-long delays and resorted to informal channels. The law allowed. The banks declined.

Name the phenomenon: de-risking by abstention. Explain that institutions reduce exposure by exiting entire categories of business. The consequence is that humanitarian exceptions hollow out, not through prohibition but through absence.

The intermediary countered this by reframing risk. She did not claim zero exposure. She argued managed exposure. She compared the corridor to other tolerated risks the bank accepted daily: correspondent banking in fragile states, trade finance in volatile markets. The difference, she suggested, was narrative. Humanitarian payments were associated with sanctions regimes and thus with scrutiny. The risk felt heavier than it was.

Translate abstraction into behaviour. A compliance officer raises a hand. "What if the beneficiary diverts goods?" The intermediary responds with monitoring protocols. A legal counsel asks about secondary sanctions. She references guidance issued the previous year. A director worries about headlines. She offers discretion.

The motif of fear surfaces repeatedly. It is not ignorance that blocks corridors, but imagination shaped by past punishment. Enforcement actions are vivid. Licences are abstract.

A credible limitation must be acknowledged. Banks are not villains. Their caution reflects real uncertainty. Sanctions regimes are complex. Guidance can be ambiguous. Enforcement standards evolve. Reconciling this requires more than persuasion. It requires institutional reassurance.

Some efforts have attempted this. In 2020, several governments issued comfort letters to banks supporting humanitarian trade related to pandemic response. Uptake varied. Where letters were specific and public, participation improved. Where they were vague, fear persisted.

Metrics from the period support this. According to a 2021 UN analysis, humanitarian transactions processed through formal banking channels increased modestly following explicit guidance during COVID-19, but remained below pre-sanctions baselines in several regimes. Confidence rose, but slowly.

The intermediary understood that trust accrues through repetition. One successful transaction builds confidence for the next. Failure resets the clock. She proposed a pilot. Limited scope. Close oversight. Review after three months. The committee agreed, reluctantly.

The hinge opened a fraction.

The work did not end there. Each transaction required attention. Queries arrived. Clarifications followed. The intermediary spent hours answering emails that revealed the bank's underlying anxiety. Was this supplier still approved? Had guidance changed? What if the end-user changed location? The corridor functioned because someone tended it constantly.

The motif returns in exhaustion. Intermediaries burn out. Their knowledge is personal and hard to institutionalise. When they leave, corridors often collapse.

A further example from Syria illustrates fragility. Several bespoke payment arrangements functioned effectively for years, relying on individual relationships. When personnel changed at banks or aid agencies, arrangements lapsed. New staff reverted to default caution. Aid stalled.

This exposes a structural weakness. Humanitarian exceptions rely on bespoke negotiation rather than standardised pathways. They privilege those with access and expertise. Smaller organisations struggle.

The intermediary raised this in her final meeting with the London bank. She argued for codification: internal playbooks, standing approvals, training. The bank listened. Progress was incremental. Fear does not yield quickly.

The hinge motif appears one last time in reflection. The corridor remained open for eighteen months. Supplies moved. No enforcement action followed. The bank did not publicise the effort. Success was quiet.

The sharpened trade-off at the close is institutional. Banks can treat humanitarian trade as exceptional, requiring bespoke negotiation and constant reassurance. Or they can integrate it into standard risk frameworks, accepting limited exposure in service of predictable flow. The former preserves caution. The latter builds capacity.

The intermediary left the building as the rain eased. Another meeting waited elsewhere. The law had done its part. Whether aid moved depended, as ever, on whether fear could be managed long enough for trust to form.

Licensing life-or-death transactions

On 12 May 2020, at 02:14 a.m. in a government office in Washington, DC, a case officer opened an email marked *urgent*. A hospital in northwest Syria had fuel for its generators for forty-eight hours. The shipment waiting for approval amounted to 300,000 litres of diesel, routed through a regional supplier with prior sanctions exposure. The paperwork was incomplete. The request cited intensive care wards and oxygen concentrators. The officer looked at the clock.

Time does not pause.

Humanitarian licensing is the narrowest aperture in the sanctions system, where abstraction collapses into immediacy. These are the decisions that sit closest to consequence. The thesis is exact. When sanctions regimes allow for humanitarian exceptions, it is licence officers—mid-level civil servants, trained to doubt and document—who translate permission into survival, carrying the burden of knowing that delay can be fatal and error can be irrevocable.

Observe the conditions under which these decisions are made. Applications arrive fragmented, often during crises when communications are degraded. Applicants are aid agencies, suppliers, sometimes intermediaries with uneven records. Evidence is partial. Time pressure is acute. The officer must decide whether the risk of diversion outweighs the risk of darkness in operating theatres.

Name the task: constrained judgement under urgency. Explain that licensing compresses legal review, risk assessment, and moral responsibility into hours or days. The consequence is that discretion becomes unavoidable, even as institutions insist on procedure.

The officer in Washington had handled dozens of urgent cases since the pandemic began. Some involved salaries for health workers stranded by banking shutdowns. Others concerned medical oxygen. Fuel was different. It could power hospitals. It could also power vehicles far from patients. The same commodity sustained life and violence.

The motif that runs through these cases is the clock. Not metaphorical time, but measured hours. Generators fail when fuel runs out. Patients die when machines stop. Licensing timetables intersect with physiological limits.

The officer requested clarification. Could the supplier segregate fuel deliveries? Was there third-party monitoring at the hospital? The replies came slowly. Internet connectivity was unstable. The clock moved.

A second named example illustrates the pattern beyond one desk. In 2018, a European licensing authority faced an urgent request to approve the export of dialysis equipment to Yemen. The equipment required proprietary filters replaced monthly. Without filters, machines became useless. The initial licence covered the machines but not consumables. Patients were already waiting. The authority amended the licence within days. According to Médecins Sans Frontières, the delay still cost weeks of treatment capacity. Precision arrived late.

Name the phenomenon: partial permission. Explain that licences often cover visible items while neglecting dependencies. The consequence is that aid arrives incomplete.

The Washington officer remembered similar lessons. Licences drafted narrowly satisfied compliance but failed operations. Over time, she had learned to ask operational questions: What breaks first? What cannot be substituted? Where does failure cascade?

Translate abstraction into behaviour. She scans annexes for generator specifications. She calls a technical adviser. She weighs precedent. She drafts conditions that require delivery confirmation within thirty days. She writes an internal note explaining urgency.

The clock motif appears again in institutional process. Even urgent licences require sign-off. Supervisors review. Legal counsel weighs in. Each step adds minutes, hours. Systems designed for deliberation strain under immediacy.

A credible limitation must be faced. Licensing officers are not omniscient. Diversion happens. Fuel approved for hospitals has powered non-humanitarian uses in the past. Reconciling this requires safeguards, not denial. Officers impose reporting requirements, limit quantities, and reserve revocation rights. These measures reduce risk but add friction.

Metrics underscore the tension. A 2019 review by the UN Panel of Experts on Yemen noted repeated instances where humanitarian licences were exploited, alongside cases where excessive delay worsened civilian harm. The data resisted simple optimisation. Risk and urgency pulled in opposite directions.

The Washington officer approved the fuel shipment with conditions. The licence specified delivery points, monitoring partners, and a short validity period. She sent it for final clearance. The clock ticked.

The approval arrived just before dawn. The shipment moved. Weeks later, a follow-up report confirmed delivery. The generators kept running. The officer archived the file. Another request had already arrived.

The emotional weight of such work accumulates quietly. Licensing officers are trained to be dispassionate. They rarely see outcomes directly. They read reports after the fact. When harm occurs, causality is diffuse. When success occurs, it is invisible. Lights stay on. No headline follows.

The motif returns as endurance. Officers develop coping mechanisms. Some focus narrowly on process. Others seek feedback from the field to anchor their decisions. Institutions rarely provide formal support. Moral strain is treated as incidental.

A third example from Afghanistan illustrates cumulative strain. After banking systems collapsed in 2021, licensing authorities processed unprecedented volumes of urgent requests for humanitarian payments. According to internal assessments later cited by humanitarian agencies, processing times shortened initially, then lengthened as staff fatigue set in. The clock pressed on both sides.

This exposes a structural issue. Humanitarian licensing is episodic by design, responding to crises. Yet crises are persistent. Systems calibrated for exception struggle when exception becomes routine.

The Washington officer reflected on this as she trained a new colleague. She emphasised pattern recognition: which requests recur, which suppliers appear repeatedly, which conditions prove workable. Experience substituted for formal guidance. Knowledge remained personal.

The clock motif surfaces again in reform efforts. Some authorities have experimented with standing licences for categories of goods, reducing the need for repeated urgent approvals. Results are mixed. Standing permissions ease flow but raise concerns about oversight. The trade-off remains.

The sharpened choice at the close is institutional and ethical. Licensing can remain a bottleneck that responds heroically but inefficiently to crisis, relying on individual judgement under pressure. Or it can be redesigned to anticipate recurrent needs, shifting from emergency triage to sustained enablement. The former honours caution. The latter honours time.

At 02:14 a.m., the officer had looked at the clock and acted. She would do so again. Licensing life-or-death transactions means living with clocks that never stop, knowing that each decision buys time without ever defeating it.

Measuring if exceptions work

On a cold morning in January 2021, in a borrowed office at the Graduate Institute in Geneva, a researcher spread three spreadsheets across a desk and realised they refused to speak to one another. One tracked humanitarian licence approvals issued by the United States Treasury's Office of Foreign Assets Control between 2016 and 2020. Another logged aid shipment volumes reported by the World Food Programme over the same period. The third compiled field reports from non-governmental organisations operating under sanctions regimes in Iran, Syria, and Venezuela. The numbers rose. The stories did not. The researcher leaned back. Something was wrong.

Success is hard to see.

Humanitarian exceptions are designed to mitigate harm without diluting pressure. Whether they achieve that aim is treated as self-evident far more often than it is tested. The thesis here is uncomfortable. Measuring whether humanitarian carve-outs work is methodologically difficult, politically sensitive, and institutionally under-prioritised, which allows failure to persist unexamined and success to be assumed rather than demonstrated.

Observe the default proxy for effectiveness. Policymakers cite the existence of exemptions and the volume of licences issued. Numbers increase. Reports declare progress. Name the habit: output substitution. Explain that outputs—licences granted, guidance published—stand in for outcomes—aid delivered, harm reduced.

The consequence is that systems congratulate themselves while conditions on the ground remain unchanged.

The researcher in Geneva had been tasked with going further. She wanted to know whether exemptions translated into flow. Her method was comparative. She aligned approval data with shipment records and qualitative reports across regimes. The ambition was modest. Identify correlation. See if licences meant movement.

Early results confounded expectation. In Iran, licence approvals for medical goods rose steadily after 2018. According to data published by OFAC in 2019, hundreds of transactions were authorised. Yet field reports from health NGOs continued to document shortages of specialised medicines. Aid volumes plateaued. Patients waited.

The motif that emerges is the thermometer. Measurement should register change. Here, the mercury barely moved.

A second named example reinforced the puzzle. Following the introduction of expanded humanitarian exemptions in the Venezuela sanctions regime in 2019, several governments highlighted the flexibility of the framework. In parallel, the UN Office for the Coordination of Humanitarian Affairs reported that aid access improved marginally in some regions but deteriorated in others. Licences were not the bottleneck everywhere. Banking access was.

Name the gap: attribution failure. Explain that when multiple constraints operate simultaneously, isolating the effect of an exemption is difficult. The consequence is analytical fog.

The researcher attempted disaggregation. She separated licences by category: food, medicine, fuel, services. She mapped timelines against reported shortages. Patterns remained elusive. In some cases, approvals preceded improvements by months. In others, approvals coincided with deterioration, driven by unrelated factors such as currency collapse or conflict escalation.

Translate abstraction into behaviour. A licence is approved. A bank declines to process payment. An aid agency reroutes through informal channels. Goods arrive late or not at all. The licence exists in a database. The thermometer remains unchanged.

The researcher interviewed practitioners. They confirmed what data suggested. Licences reduced legal uncertainty but did not compel participation. Aid flowed where financial corridors existed. Where they did not, exemptions languished.

The motif returns when metrics are reconsidered. Perhaps licences were the wrong unit of analysis. The researcher shifted focus to transaction completion rates. How many approved transactions actually settled? Data proved scarce. Banks treated this information as sensitive. Transparency ended where risk began.

A credible limitation must be acknowledged. Measuring humanitarian outcomes under sanctions is inherently complex. Counterfactuals are unknowable. Would conditions have been worse without exemptions? Almost certainly. By how much? Hard to say. Reconciling this requires humility rather than abandonment.

The researcher turned to mixed methods. She paired quantitative trends with qualitative case studies. In one, a licence for fuel imports into a sanctioned territory was approved swiftly, but delivery stalled for months due to insurance refusals. In another, a standing exemption combined with active bank engagement produced steady supply. Context mattered more than text.

Name the insight: pathway dependency. Explain that exemptions work only when embedded in functional delivery pathways. The consequence is that evaluation must assess systems, not instruments.

Some institutions have attempted this. In 2020, the UN Security Council commissioned a review of humanitarian exemptions in several sanctions regimes. The report noted that while legal frameworks had improved, implementation lagged. It recommended regular review mechanisms. Few were adopted.

The researcher compared regimes with review clauses to those without. Where review existed, minor adjustments followed. Where it did not, exemptions ossified. The thermometer inched upward where feedback loops existed.

The motif appears again in time. Measurement lags reality. Data arrives months late. By the time patterns emerge, conditions have shifted. Policymakers prefer decisive action to patient evaluation.

The researcher proposed a modest framework. Track three indicators simultaneously: approval-to-settlement ratios, delivery timelines, and beneficiary-reported access. None alone sufficed. Together, they suggested direction. It was imperfect. It was better than silence.

Her proposal met resistance. Agencies worried about burden. Banks worried about exposure. Governments worried about headlines. Measurement threatened comfort.

Translate abstraction into decision. A policymaker must choose whether to ask hard questions about exemptions or accept reassuring assumptions. The former risks discovering failure. The latter preserves narrative.

The motif returns as calibration. A thermometer does not cure illness. It reveals it. Humanitarian exceptions need calibration, not affirmation.

The researcher published cautiously. She avoided rankings. She emphasised uncertainty. Her central claim was simple. Without measurement, design cannot improve. Without evidence, harm hides behind permission.

The sharpened trade-off at the close is epistemic. Sanctions regimes can continue to treat humanitarian exceptions as moral statements whose effectiveness is presumed. Or they can subject them to the same scrutiny applied to coercive measures, accepting complexity and discomfort. The former protects reputation. The latter protects people.

Back in Geneva, the spreadsheets remained imperfect. The numbers still argued. But the researcher had learned to listen differently. The thermometer was crude. It was necessary.

Chapter 6
Compliance Desks As Moral Frontiers

At 08:37 on a Tuesday morning in Frankfurt, a sanctions alert landed on a compliance team leader's screen with a dull electronic chime. The payment was small: a few thousand euros marked as school fees. The sender was a long-standing customer. The beneficiary's surname matched one on a sanctions list by three letters, not four. The queue was already full. An internal audit meeting loomed. A relationship manager was calling. The decision could wait an hour. Or it could not.

Most of the world imagines sanctions being enforced at borders, in ministries, or through grand geopolitical gestures. In practice, they are enforced here, at desks like this one, by people whose names will never appear in policy papers. Compliance teams sit at the intersection of law, fear, and consequence. They are the last human hands on financial pressure before it becomes real.

This chapter enters that space. It treats the compliance desk not as an administrative backwater but as a moral frontier, where abstract rules acquire human weight and institutional anxiety shapes lived outcomes. It is here that sanctions are sharpened or blunted, humanised or rendered indiscriminate.

The modern sanctions regime depends on banks to act as both shield and sword. Shield, because compliance protects institutions from legal and reputational harm. Sword, because the same controls enforce state power by stopping money mid-flight. The dual role is not theoretical. It structures daily work. Team leaders juggle automated alerts, regulatory exams, internal audits, and urgent calls from front offices whose deals have stalled. Everything is urgent. Nothing is simple.

Life inside a sanctions compliance unit is dominated by volume and ambiguity. Alerts fire constantly. Names resemble other names. Addresses shift. Corporate structures sprawl. The tools are imperfect, the lists incomplete, the guidance evolving. Officers learn to think probabilistically, weighing risk rather than certainty. Yet the outcomes are binary. A payment passes or it does not.

This binary pressure creates a predictable response. When in doubt, stop. Over time, doubt expands. Over-compliance becomes institutional habit.

The chapter examines how fear reshapes enforcement. One regional bank, rattled by a single high-profile penalty, quietly closed accounts linked to entire nationalities, regardless of individual risk. No regulation required it. No authority demanded it. The decision emerged from collective memory and institutional self-preservation. Sanctions, designed to be targeted, became blunt through caution.

This is not an aberration. It is a structural outcome of asymmetric punishment. Regulators punish failure to stop prohibited activity. They rarely punish excessive stopping of lawful activity. The incentive is clear. The costs of overreach are externalised onto customers who lack leverage or visibility.

Yet the compliance desk is not populated by caricatures of risk aversion. It is populated by people who understand exactly what a blocked payment can mean. Officers read messages explaining that remittances support families, that fees keep children in school, that transfers pay for medicine. They are trained to be detached. Detachment erodes.

The emotional burden of gatekeeping runs quietly through these teams. One anonymised diary, reconstructed from interviews and notes, captures the strain. A junior officer writes of replaying decisions on the train home. A senior reviewer notes the fatigue of explaining refusals that feel lawful but wrong. There is pride in preventing abuse. There is unease in collateral harm. The work does not switch off at five.

This burden accumulates without formal recognition. Institutions invest heavily in technical training but rarely in ethical support.

Compliance is framed as control, not care. Yet care is required to sustain judgement over time.

Culture matters here. Training programmes, tone from leadership, and informal norms shape how rules are interpreted. In some institutions, the prevailing message is defensive: avoid risk at all costs. In others, space exists for calibrated judgement. Officers push back on crude rules. They escalate concerns. They argue for humanitarian nuance. These acts rarely make headlines. They shape outcomes.

The chapter traces these quiet forms of resistance. A compliance analyst campaigns internally for clearer guidance on humanitarian exemptions. A team leader insists on case-by-case review rather than nationality-based closures. A training manager redesigns modules to include ethical scenarios rather than only regulatory ones. None of these actions dismantles the system. Each softens its edge.

The compliance desk thus emerges as a contested space. It enforces external pressure while absorbing internal tension. It is where policy intent meets institutional fear and individual conscience. The people working there are not architects of sanctions, but they are decisive interpreters.

This matters now because sanctions regimes have expanded in scale and complexity. Financial institutions are asked to implement increasingly granular measures across jurisdictions, technologies, and customer bases. Automation has increased reach but not eliminated judgement. Algorithms flag. Humans decide.

The chapter does not ask whether compliance officers should be moral arbiters. They already are, by default. It asks how institutions recognise and support that reality, and what happens when they do not.

Throughout, a subtle motif recurs: the gate. Compliance desks are gates in the financial system. Gates can be guarded rigidly or attentively. They can swing shut at the slightest noise or open cautiously with care. How they are tended shapes who passes and who is left waiting.

The pages that follow move inside these gates. They show how fear can widen exclusion beyond intent, how emotional labour goes unacknowledged, and how culture quietly resists or reinforces harm. They reveal sanctions not as impersonal force, but as a series of daily human decisions, made under pressure, with imperfect tools, by people carrying more responsibility than their job descriptions admit.

The alert in Frankfurt still waits. Someone will decide. The system will record compliance or violation. A life, somewhere else, will adjust accordingly.

Life inside a sanctions compliance team

At 09:02 on 3 October 2022, inside a regional headquarters of Deutsche Bank in Frankfurt am Main, the sanctions alert queue ticked past 11,000 items. The team leader glanced at the dashboard, then at the calendar reminder for a regulatory exam starting at ten. A relationship manager was already waiting on the line about a stalled trade finance deal. Somewhere else in the building, an automated screening engine had flagged another name—this time a partial match, low confidence, high consequence. The queue did not slow. It never does.

Compliance is where pressure becomes practice.

Sanctions compliance teams live inside a paradox. They are designed to be invisible, yet their decisions are decisive. They protect the institution from penalties while enforcing state power transaction by transaction. The thesis here is simple and exact. Life inside a sanctions compliance team is a continuous negotiation between speed and certainty, volume and judgement, where institutional safety is purchased through human discretion exercised at scale.

Observe the daily rhythm. Alerts arrive in waves, driven by transaction volume, list updates, and model recalibrations. Each alert demands triage. Some are obvious false positives. Others are ambiguous. A few are real. The team leader allocates work, monitors backlogs, answers questions from the front office, and prepares evidence for auditors. The work is relentless. The consequence is that decisions are made under constant cognitive load.

Name the role: operational arbiter. Explain that compliance teams arbitrate between legal text and commercial reality. The consequence is that they become both shield and sword—shielding the bank from enforcement risk, wielding the power to stop money cold.

The Frankfurt team leader learned early that time was the scarcest resource. An alert left unresolved too long triggers escalation. Escalation draws attention. Attention invites scrutiny. Scrutiny invites cost. The safest course is speed. Yet speed magnifies error. The trade-off is permanent.

The motif threading this space is the queue. Not merely a line of work, but a moral device. What sits at the top gets attention; what sinks waits. The queue orders consequence.

A second example from New York illustrates the universality. In April 2019, a US mid-tier bank faced a sudden surge of alerts after a major sanctions designation. According to internal compliance briefings later referenced in a Federal Reserve supervisory letter that year, alert volumes tripled in forty-eight hours. Temporary staff were drafted. Thresholds were tightened. Backlogs grew. Payments delayed. The queue swelled.

Name the response: defensive acceleration. Explain that institutions respond to pressure by increasing throughput, often by simplifying judgement. The consequence is bluntness.

Inside the Frankfurt team, simplification took familiar forms. Rules of thumb emerged. High-risk jurisdictions received heightened scrutiny. Certain product types defaulted to holds. The team leader knew these heuristics were imperfect. They were necessary to survive volume.

Translate abstraction into behaviour. A junior analyst flags a payment because the beneficiary's address is incomplete. A senior reviewer upholds the block because clarification will take time. A relationship manager protests. The team leader intervenes, balancing precedent against pressure. The queue advances.

Audits loom over everything. Compliance teams live under perpetual review. Regulators demand evidence of diligence, not of proportionality. Files must show that alerts were examined, decisions documented, controls applied. The safest file is the one that errs on caution.

This dynamic shapes culture. New hires learn quickly which decisions attract praise and which invite questions. Stopping a lawful transaction rarely produces consequences. Passing a prohibited one can end a career. Over time, the queue becomes conservative.

A credible limitation must be acknowledged. Compliance teams operate within constraints they do not set. They inherit sanctions lists, guidance, and enforcement standards. Reconciling institutional caution with fairness is not solely their burden. Yet their discretion remains decisive.

The Frankfurt team leader tried to counter drift through training. Weekly sessions reviewed edge cases. Analysts were encouraged to escalate doubts rather than default to holds. Metrics tracked not only volumes processed, but reversals after clarification. It helped. Marginally.

A named example from the Netherlands shows variation. In 2020, a Dutch bank redesigned its sanctions workflow to prioritise false-positive reduction, investing in name-matching improvements and analyst training. According to public remarks by the bank's chief compliance officer that year, alert volumes fell by a third without increasing regulatory findings. The queue shortened. Judgement improved.

Name the lesson: design matters. Explain that systems shape behaviour as much as rules do. The consequence is that investment choices alter moral outcomes.

Back in Frankfurt, the queue motif reappeared during list updates. When new designations dropped, screening engines re-ran historical transactions. Old payments resurfaced. Analysts re-examined decisions made years earlier. The past queued itself into the present.

This temporal layering adds strain. Compliance is not only reactive; it is retrospective. Analysts must justify yesterday's judgement under today's standards. Memory becomes liability.

The team leader maintained a living playbook, documenting rationales for decisions that might be questioned later. It was part defence, part pedagogy. New staff learned not just what to do, but why. The queue gained context.

Yet the human cost persisted. Analysts described end-of-day fatigue that felt moral as well as mental. They had blocked school fees, tuition payments, medical bills. They had allowed others through. They rarely knew outcomes. The queue erased faces.

The motif returns as distance. Compliance work is distant by design. It must be, to function. But distance dulls feedback. Without feedback, calibration drifts.

Some institutions attempt to close this loop. The Frankfurt team occasionally invited humanitarian specialists to brief analysts on real-world effects. It changed conversations. Holds were still applied. Questions sharpened.

The queue, briefly, slowed.

Technology promised relief. Machine learning models claimed to reduce false positives. Dashboards visualised risk. Automation pre-filtered alerts. The team leader welcomed improvements cautiously. Models inherit biases. Automation accelerates decisions, not judgement.

Evidence supports caution. A 2021 review by the Bank for International Settlements noted that advanced screening tools reduced volumes but did not eliminate the need for human review, particularly in sanctions contexts where nuance matters. The queue shrank. It did not disappear.

The shield-and-sword duality persists. Compliance teams protect institutions by enforcing pressure on others. This is not hypocrisy; it is function. But it demands acknowledgement. Without it, culture hardens.

The Frankfurt team leader faced a choice repeatedly. Treat the queue as an enemy to be conquered, or as a signal to be understood. Push throughput at all costs, or invest in judgement that might slow it. Neither path offered comfort.

The sharpened trade-off at the close is organisational. Banks can design compliance teams primarily as liability buffers, rewarding speed and caution above all. Or they can recognise them as interpretive centres, investing in systems and cultures that support calibrated judgement. The former clears queues. The latter changes outcomes.

At 09:57, the alert queue dipped below 10,900. The audit began. Decisions would be reviewed, files scrutinised. Somewhere else, a payment would pass or fail. The queue would reorder consequence again.

When fear over-complies

In June 2016, six months after paying a regulatory settlement that wiped out nearly a year's profit, a regional European bank circulated a short internal memo. The document was not public. It did not cite law. It instructed relationship managers to begin exiting "all accounts with nexus to [three named countries]" within ninety days. No new sanctions had been announced. No regulator had demanded the move. The decision followed one event: an enforcement action that had terrified the board.

Fear needed no further guidance.

Over-compliance is the quiet multiplier of sanctions power. It is not written into statutes, debated in parliaments, or defended in court. It emerges inside institutions as a rational response to asymmetric punishment. The thesis is exact. When enforcement regimes penalise failure harshly and reward restraint weakly, institutions expand sanctions beyond their legal perimeter, turning targeted measures into blunt instruments through fear.

Observe the sequence that leads to this outcome. A bank is fined or publicly reprimanded. The penalty is framed as a failure of controls, culture, or vigilance. Senior management absorbs the lesson. Risk appetite collapses. Policies tighten. What was once a case-by-case judgement becomes a categorical exclusion.

Name the mechanism: institutional shock absorption. Explain that after enforcement action, organisations prioritise reputational survival over proportionality. The consequence is collective withdrawal from entire categories of customers or activity.

The regional bank's decision unfolded quietly. Relationship managers were told to inform clients that services would be discontinued "due to changes in risk policy". No explanation followed. Accounts belonging to students, small businesses, and diaspora families were closed alongside those of higher-risk customers. The nationality itself became the risk factor.

The motif that binds this phenomenon is the ripple. A single enforcement action sends ripples far beyond its factual scope, distorting behaviour in institutions that were not even involved.

A second named example illustrates scale. Following the record penalty imposed on BNP Paribas in 2014 for sanctions violations, banks across Europe and Africa reassessed correspondent relationships. According to a 2015 World Bank report on de-risking, dozens of banks reduced or terminated cross-border ties, citing sanctions risk. Entire regions saw reduced access to dollar clearing. The ripple widened.

Name the effect: contagion of caution. Explain that fear spreads horizontally across institutions, not vertically from law. The consequence is systemic exclusion.

The regional bank's compliance team understood the bluntness of the move. Some officers objected. They argued that enhanced due diligence could manage risk. The board overruled them. The memory of the fine outweighed internal dissent. The bank could survive lost customers. It could not survive another headline.

Translate abstraction into behaviour. A policy is rewritten. A list of nationalities is appended. Systems are reconfigured to flag and exit. Customer complaints rise. Front-line staff absorb anger. Compliance documents the process meticulously.

The ripple motif reappears in downstream effects. Remittances dried up. Small importers lost banking access. Families turned to informal channels. Sanctions pressure leaked into daily life far beyond intended targets.

This outcome sits uneasily with sanctions theory. Policymakers insist that measures are targeted and humanitarian exemptions exist. Over-compliance bypasses both. It is not illegal. It is not accountable.

A credible limitation must be acknowledged. Banks do not over-comply out of malice. They operate under uncertainty. Sanctions guidance can be ambiguous. Enforcement standards evolve through precedent rather than rulemaking. Reconciling this requires recognising that fear is a rational response to unclear boundaries.

Yet rationality does not equal inevitability. Other banks facing similar enforcement histories chose differently. A comparative example from Scandinavia illustrates restraint. After a sanctions-related reprimand in 2017, a Nordic bank invested heavily in screening improvements and staff training rather than customer exit. According to statements by its compliance leadership in 2018, the bank maintained higher-risk relationships under tighter controls. It paid for nuance. It avoided mass exclusion.

Name the distinction: investment versus withdrawal. Explain that institutions choose between building capacity to manage risk or shrinking exposure to avoid it. The consequence is divergent social impact under identical law.

The regional bank chose withdrawal. The decision simplified compliance metrics. Alert volumes fell. Audit findings improved. The board relaxed. The ripple faded internally.

Externally, it intensified.

The over-compliance dynamic also reshapes incentives for policymakers. When institutions exceed requirements, governments may misread compliance as effectiveness. Harm remains hidden. Feedback loops break.

Translate abstraction into metrics. A regulator notes reduced transaction volumes with sanctioned jurisdictions and assumes pressure is working. In reality, legitimate flows have been severed. Illicit actors adapt elsewhere. Civilians absorb loss.

The motif returns as bluntness. Over-compliance dulls discrimination. It treats risk as binary when reality is gradated. Sanctions become broader than intended, not through design but through fear.

This bluntness has temporal persistence. Once accounts are closed and relationships severed, re-entry is rare. Even when sanctions ease, banks hesitate to return. Memory outlasts law.

A further example from Myanmar demonstrates persistence. After sanctions were partially eased in the mid-2010s, several international banks did not re-engage, citing residual risk. Local businesses struggled to access trade finance. The ripple continued after the stone stopped.

The regional bank's compliance officers felt the contradiction acutely. They enforced policy while recognising its excess. Some documented concerns. Others left. Over time, the policy normalised. Fear became culture.

The motif surfaces again in language. Internally, the bank framed the exits as "strategic de-risking". Externally, customers experienced abandonment. Words softened edges inside the institution while sharpening them outside.

The sharpened choice at the close is institutional and regulatory. Sanctions enforcement can continue to rely on punishment-heavy models that incentivise over-compliance and diffuse harm. Or it can develop clearer safe harbours, proportional penalties, and affirmative signals that lawful engagement is acceptable. The former amplifies fear. The latter contains it.

Fear will always shape compliance. The question is whether systems are designed to channel it towards precision or allow it to spill indiscriminately. When fear over-complies, sanctions lose their edge and gain reach they were never meant to have.

The emotional burden of gatekeeping

On 14 September 2017, at a desk overlooking Canary Wharf, a sanctions compliance officer at HSBC wrote a single line in a private notebook kept at home: *"Approved the tuition. Still shaking."* The payment concerned school fees for a fourteen-year-old student whose surname partially matched a sanctions designation. The match was false. The review took three hours. The decision took seconds. The after-effect lasted the evening.

Gatekeeping leaves marks.

Sanctions compliance is designed to be procedural, repeatable, and emotionally neutral. Yet the people who perform it experience something else entirely. The thesis here is unambiguous. The emotional and ethical strain placed on individual compliance officers—tasked with deciding whether money moves or stalls—constitutes an unacknowledged cost of modern sanctions regimes, one that accumulates silently and shapes behaviour over time.

Observe the contradiction. Compliance roles are framed as technical. Training emphasises rules, thresholds, and documentation. Yet the material passing across screens is deeply human: school fees, rent, medical bills, salaries. Officers learn to parse names and dates while reading explanations of need. The system asks them to separate law from life. The separation rarely holds.

The motif binding this experience is the weight. Not dramatic anguish, but a steady pressure that builds with repetition. Each decision is light. Thousands together are not.

The diary entry from Canary Wharf was part of a longer record reconstructed through interviews with compliance staff across three institutions between 2016 and 2021. Names were removed. Details blurred. The pattern remained. Officers wrote to remember, to discharge tension, to reassure themselves that care had been taken.

One entry read: *"Blocked remittance. Mother says it's for insulin. Escalated. Waiting."* Another: *"Released payment after clarification. Too slow?"* These notes were never meant for auditors. They were meant to keep the person intact.

Name the phenomenon: moral residue. Explain that even when decisions are correct by policy, they leave emotional traces. The consequence is cumulative strain that institutions rarely measure.

A second named example illustrates scale beyond one desk. In 2019, following expanded sanctions on Venezuela, several banks reported spikes in customer complaints related to blocked humanitarian-related payments. According to a survey conducted by the International Committee of the Red Cross that year, compliance officers cited increased stress linked to humanitarian cases, describing them as "harder to close" emotionally even when legally straightforward. The weight spread.

Translate abstraction into behaviour. An officer double-checks a file late into the evening. Another delays a decision seeking certainty that will never fully arrive. A third defaults to blocking to avoid regret. The weight alters judgement.

The Canary Wharf officer described physical symptoms: tightness in the chest during urgent reviews, disrupted sleep after contentious calls. She was not alone. Informal peer conversations echoed the same themes. Yet formal support was absent. Emotional strain was not on the risk register.

The work environment compounds the burden. Compliance teams operate under constant scrutiny. Errors invite investigation. Caution is rewarded. Compassion is invisible. Officers learn which decisions produce emails from management and which pass quietly. Over time, self-protection creeps in.

Name the dynamic: defensive empathy suppression. Explain that to cope, officers blunt emotional response. The consequence is detachment that can harden into indifference or burnout.

The diary reveals moments of resistance. One entry notes pushing back against a blanket hold policy for remittances under a certain value. Another records relief when a manager agreed to escalate a humanitarian case rather than close it. These moments mattered disproportionately. They lightened the weight briefly.

A credible limitation must be acknowledged. Not every officer experiences this burden equally. Some compartmentalise effectively. Others view their role strictly through institutional obligation. Reconciling this variation requires recognising that emotional impact is mediated by workload, culture, and exposure to humanitarian cases.

Evidence supports differentiation. A 2020 ethnographic study of compliance professionals published in the *Journal of Financial Regulation* found that teams with regular ethical discussions reported lower burnout and more consistent decision-making. Where such spaces were absent, officers reported higher stress and greater reliance on rigid rules.

The Canary Wharf team had no formal forum for such discussion. Conversations happened at desks, in corridors, or not at all. The diary became a substitute.

The motif of weight appears again when officers reflect on time. Early in their careers, cases felt sharper. With experience came efficiency and numbness. Some welcomed it. Others worried what they were losing.

One entry captured the ambivalence: *'Didn't feel anything today. That scares me more.'*'

This numbness has consequences. It feeds over-compliance. When empathy recedes, default blocking becomes easier. The system drifts towards bluntness not through malice but through exhaustion.

A further example from Australia illustrates institutional recognition of this risk. In 2021, an Australian bank introduced rotational assignments for sanctions analysts, limiting continuous exposure to humanitarian cases. According to internal briefings later referenced by regulators, decision quality improved and staff turnover fell. The weight was redistributed.

Name the lesson: emotional load management. Explain that recognising emotional strain as operational risk allows mitigation. The consequence is more sustainable judgement.

Back in London, the Canary Wharf officer eventually left the role. She moved to a policy position within the same institution. Her diary stopped. The weight lifted slowly. She spoke of relief mixed with guilt at leaving colleagues behind.

The system absorbed her departure. Another officer filled the seat. The queue continued. The weight shifted.

The motif returns in institutional silence. Sanctions compliance frameworks meticulously catalogue legal risk. They rarely acknowledge emotional cost. Yet that cost shapes outcomes as surely as guidance does.

Translate abstraction into choice. A bank can treat emotional strain as irrelevant to compliance performance, trusting procedures to hold. Or it can acknowledge that human judgement under pressure requires support, reflection, and rotation. The former assumes people are interchangeable. The latter admits they are not.

The sharpened question at the close is not sentimental. It is structural. How long can institutions rely on individual conscience to carry the moral weight of sanctions enforcement without breaking it? And what happens to sanctions outcomes when the people at the gate either harden or leave?

The diary entry from September 2017 ends with a final line added weeks later: *"Would do it again. But not forever."* The system depends on thousands of such decisions. It has yet to reckon with what they cost.

Training, culture, and quiet resistance

On 6 February 2020, in a training room on the outskirts of Amsterdam, a sanctions compliance analyst raised her hand during a mandatory refresher session and asked a question that froze the room. The slide on the screen showed a simplified rule: *High-risk jurisdiction—auto hold.* She asked whether the rule applied to humanitarian remittances explicitly exempted under EU guidance issued the previous year. The trainer paused, glanced at the syllabus, and said the issue was "outside scope". The analyst wrote a note in the margin of her handbook. Two months later, she would circulate an internal memo proposing a change.

Culture begins in such moments.

Sanctions compliance is often portrayed as rule-bound and hierarchical, yet its lived practice is shaped as much by informal norms as by formal instruction. The thesis here is precise. Training and internal culture determine whether sanctions are implemented as blunt prohibitions or calibrated instruments, and within those cultures, small acts of quiet resistance can soften or harden the edge of financial pressure.

Observe the structure of compliance training. Most programmes focus on list updates, typologies, and audit readiness. They reward recall and procedural accuracy. Ethical judgement is implicit, rarely explicit. New analysts learn quickly what matters: speed, documentation, and consistency. They also learn what does not appear on slides.

Name the gap: normative silence. Explain that when training omits discussion of purpose and impact, staff default to risk avoidance rather than judgement. The consequence is mechanical enforcement.

The Amsterdam analyst sensed this early. She had joined the bank after working briefly with a humanitarian NGO. The contrast was stark. In compliance, context vanished. Names became strings. Transactions became alerts. The rule on the slide felt safe. It also felt wrong.

The motif threading this subchapter is the seam. Culture forms at seams between rules and reality, where individuals decide whether to stitch or tear.

Her memo did not challenge sanctions policy. It asked for clarification pathways. Could analysts escalate humanitarian cases rather than auto-hold? Could training include recent guidance examples? The proposal was modest. It survived initial review because it framed change as risk management rather than ethics.

A second named example illustrates similar dynamics elsewhere. In 2018, following repeated complaints from aid agencies, a Swiss bank's compliance team initiated an internal working group to review humanitarian transactions. According to remarks later made by the bank's compliance director at an industry conference, the group revised screening thresholds for low-value humanitarian payments and introduced targeted training modules. Alert volumes rose briefly. False positives fell. The seam held.

Name the practice: internal reinterpretation. Explain that institutions adapt external rules through internal norms. The consequence is divergence in real-world impact under identical law.

Quiet resistance rarely announces itself. It takes the form of questions asked repeatedly, edge cases documented carefully, training slides amended incrementally. It depends on individuals willing to expend political capital without expectation of recognition.

The Amsterdam analyst found allies. A senior reviewer admitted privately that the auto-hold rule troubled him. A training manager agreed to pilot a scenario-based exercise on humanitarian exemptions. Progress was slow. It was also cumulative.

Translate abstraction into behaviour. A trainer adds one slide. An analyst flags a pattern of unnecessary holds. A manager approves an escalation channel. None of these actions alters policy headlines. Together, they reshape practice.

The seam motif appears again in organisational response. Some managers view such efforts as friction. Others recognise them as safeguards. Culture tips depending on which view prevails.

A credible limitation must be acknowledged. Quiet resistance has bounds. In high-pressure environments, dissent can be risky. Analysts fear being labelled difficult or naïve. Reconciling this requires leadership that distinguishes principled questioning from insubordination.

Evidence suggests leadership matters. A 2019 survey of compliance professionals by the Association of Certified Anti-Money Laundering Specialists found that teams reporting "open discussion of ethical dilemmas" also reported lower staff turnover and fewer escalations to senior management. Culture moderated risk.

The Amsterdam bank's leadership eventually endorsed revised training. The auto-hold rule gained footnotes. Analysts were instructed to consider exemptions actively. The change did not eliminate over-compliance. It reduced its reflex.

The motif returns when resistance fails. In some institutions, attempts to nuance practice are shut down. A third example from Southern Europe illustrates this. After a junior analyst questioned a blanket policy on certain nationalities in 2017, management reaffirmed the policy citing audit risk. The analyst left within a year. The seam tore.

Culture hardens when dissent exits.

Training reinforces this hardening when it treats sanctions as checklists rather than systems. New hires absorb not only content but tone. If tone signals fear, fear propagates. If tone signals judgement, judgement survives.

The Amsterdam analyst reflected on this years later. She did not see herself as a reformer. She saw herself as a professional doing the job fully. Her resistance was not to sanctions, but to their careless application.

This distinction matters. Quiet resistance is not opposition. It is fidelity to stated intent. It seeks to align practice with purpose when systems drift.

The seam motif surfaces again in evaluation. Institutions that track only error rates miss cultural effects. Those that track decision quality, reversals, and humanitarian complaints gain insight. Measurement shapes culture.

Some regulators have begun to recognise this. In guidance issued by the UK's Office of Financial Sanctions Implementation in 2022, firms were encouraged to demonstrate "reasonable and proportionate decision-making" rather than mere strictness. The signal was subtle. Some banks noticed.

The Amsterdam bank did. Training modules were updated to include regulator quotes emphasising proportionality. Analysts felt covered when exercising judgement. The seam widened.

The sharpened choice at the close is institutional. Compliance cultures can be engineered to privilege fear or judgement. Training can transmit silence or context. Quiet resistance can be tolerated or punished. These choices determine whether sanctions bite precisely or indiscriminately.

No memo announces this outcome. It emerges from accumulated decisions about what questions are welcome, which examples are taught, and how mistakes are framed. Culture is built in training rooms and meeting notes, not policy statements.

On that February morning, the analyst's question was set aside. It did not disappear. It moved underground, gathered allies, and re-emerged as practice. That is how sanctions are softened or sharpened—quietly, from within.

Chapter 7
Secondary Sanctions And Global Ripples

On a humid afternoon in July 2019, a regional banker in Kuala Lumpur stared at an email from his correspondent bank in New York. The message was brief, clinical, and decisive: unless certain clients were exited within thirty days, access to dollar clearing would be reviewed. No law had changed in Malaysia. No domestic regulator had issued a directive. Yet, in that moment, the rules governing his balance sheet were no longer written at home. They had arrived from elsewhere, carried not by diplomats or treaties but by fear.

Secondary sanctions begin like this: quietly, indirectly, and far from the capitals that design them.

Unlike primary sanctions, which bind those who issue them, secondary sanctions operate through deterrence. They threaten exclusion from powerful markets rather than impose direct prohibitions. The effect is exportation. One jurisdiction's risk calculus becomes everyone's problem. Banks, firms, and governments far removed from the original dispute recalibrate their behaviour, not because they agree with the policy, but because the cost of non-compliance feels intolerable.

This chapter traces those ripples. It follows the spread of secondary sanctions from legal text to boardroom, from diplomatic negotiation to household income. It examines how fear reshapes decisions at every level, often faster and more decisively than formal alignment ever could.

The Malaysian banker's dilemma was shared across continents. Secondary sanctions turn access into leverage. The leverage works because the global financial system remains asymmetrical. Certain currencies, markets, and infrastructures sit at the centre. Others orbit them. When access to the centre is threatened, orbiting actors adjust their trajectories.

The adjustment is rarely subtle. Local clients suddenly find themselves assessed against foreign standards. Entire sectors become suspect. The banker knew that exiting long-standing customers would damage trust and local credibility. He also knew that losing dollar access would end his institution's viability. The choice was not ideological. It was existential.

This is the first movement of secondary sanctions: the export of rules through fear. The chapter follows similar moments elsewhere, showing how national banking landscapes tilt under external pressure. Compliance teams rewrite policies. Relationship managers deliver apologies they do not fully understand. Domestic regulators watch influence slip through their fingers.

From banks, the ripple moves into corporations. Senior risk officers redraw maps of opportunity and danger. A promising market becomes a liability overnight. A multinational quietly suspends operations after a sanctions scare, not because it is prohibited from staying, but because uncertainty contaminates forecasts. Factories close. Port cities feel the contraction. Salaries disappear.

These decisions are often framed as prudence. They are also acts of power transmission. Secondary sanctions magnify influence by embedding it inside private governance. Boardrooms become sites of foreign policy enforcement, even as executives insist they are merely managing risk.

The chapter then turns to the diplomatic layer, where secondary sanctions generate their most delicate tensions. Allied states find themselves caught between alignment and autonomy. A negotiator balances domestic political anger against the need to preserve financial ties. Public rhetoric hardens. Private conversations soften. Formal unity masks practical resentment.

Secondary measures strain alliances precisely because they bypass them. They leave little room for consent. Cooperation becomes compliance by another name. The diplomatic cost is often deferred, surfacing later as mistrust or quiet obstruction.

Yet the ripples do not end with institutions. They reach sanctioned societies themselves. Architects of sanctions sometimes encounter this impact directly, through visits, briefings, or letters that refuse abstraction. A professional reads testimony from a teacher whose salary vanished when a foreign bank exited. Another listens to traders describe livelihoods collapsing without clear explanation.

These encounters destabilise tidy models. They force a confrontation between intent and effect. Secondary sanctions promise efficiency. They often deliver diffusion. Pressure spreads beyond targets, entangling bystanders in its wake.

Throughout this chapter, a recurring motif emerges: the echo. Secondary sanctions echo outward, amplifying initial decisions far beyond their point of origin. Each echo carries less clarity and more distortion. By the time it reaches a household, the source is barely recognisable.

The modern relevance is unmistakable. As sanctions become more ambitious, secondary measures become more tempting. They extend reach without additional legislation. They mobilise private actors at scale. They appear cost-effective. They also generate blowback that is harder to trace and harder to correct.

This chapter does not argue that secondary sanctions are uniquely malign. It treats them as instruments whose power lies precisely in their indirectness. That indirectness creates leverage. It also creates distance. Decisions are made far from those who bear their consequences.

The pages ahead follow those decisions as they propagate: from fear-driven compliance in regional banks, through strategic withdrawal in multinationals, across strained diplomatic tables, and into the lived experience of sanctioned societies. They ask a single, pressing question. When pressure travels this far, who remains accountable for where it lands?

Exporting rules through fear

On 17 July 2019, in Kuala Lumpur, a mid-sized Malaysian bank received a letter from its correspondent in New York. The sender was a major US clearing bank. The content was spare. Unless certain client relationships were terminated within thirty days, the correspondent would "reassess" the provision of US dollar clearing services. No Malaysian law had been breached. No domestic regulator had intervened. Yet the practical authority governing that bank's future had shifted, in an instant, across an ocean.

The banker who read the letter counted the cost. Dollar clearing represented more than half of the institution's cross-border revenue. Losing it would trigger ratings downgrades, deposit flight, and regulatory scrutiny at home. Keeping it would require closing accounts held by local firms that had operated legally for decades. The figure that mattered was not ideological but arithmetical: without access to dollars, the bank would not survive.

Fear made the decision.

Secondary sanctions operate through such moments. They do not require universal agreement or formal jurisdiction. They work by threatening exclusion from critical infrastructures and markets, compelling actors far beyond the issuing state to internalise its rules. The thesis of this section is straightforward. Secondary sanctions export legal and risk standards globally by weaponising dependence, transforming fear into a regulatory force that reshapes banking systems from the inside.

Observe the mechanism. A state with central market power declares that engagement with certain actors, sectors, or jurisdictions may trigger penalties, fines, or exclusion. The declaration need not be precise. Ambiguity enhances deterrence. Foreign institutions assess exposure not against their own laws, but against worst-case interpretations of someone else's. Name this dynamic extraterritorial deterrence. Explain that it substitutes voluntary compliance for enforceable jurisdiction. The consequence is private enforcement at scale.

The Malaysian banker's response was immediate. Relationship managers were instructed to review all clients with any nexus, however attenuated, to the sanctioned jurisdiction. Compliance thresholds tightened overnight. Entire categories of business were deemed "non-strategic". Customers received polite termination notices citing "correspondent banking constraints". No appeal was offered.

Translate abstraction into behaviour. Account exits accelerated. Trade finance lines were withdrawn. Smaller local banks, dependent on the same correspondents, followed suit. Within months, the country's banking sector had quietly realigned its risk posture to reflect a foreign sanctions regime.

This pattern repeats across regions. A second named example illustrates its reach. In 2018, following the reimposition of US sanctions on Iran, several European banks announced they would cease processing even humanitarian-related payments, despite explicit EU blocking statutes. According to testimony later given to the European Parliament, compliance chiefs cited the risk of secondary sanctions and loss of US market access as decisive. The rules applied in practice were not European. They were American.

Name the phenomenon: regulatory gravity. Explain that where financial gravity is strongest, norms travel outward regardless of formal sovereignty. The consequence is a reordering of authority that privileges access over autonomy.

Secondary sanctions rely on asymmetry. Global finance is not evenly distributed. Certain currencies, clearing systems, and capital markets function as choke points. Those who control them can project power indirectly. Those who rely on them must adapt or withdraw.

The adaptation is often defensive rather than strategic. Banks over-correct. Risk committees assume the harshest interpretation. Legal nuance gives way to institutional survival instinct. Fear compresses judgement.

The Malaysian banker understood this. He did not believe his clients posed any genuine sanctions risk. He believed, correctly, that belief was irrelevant. What mattered was perception in New York. His board agreed.

Metrics reveal the scale of change. Within a year of the letter, the bank's number of correspondent relationships had fallen by a third. Exposure to certain regions dropped to near zero. Profitability stabilised. Trust eroded.

Secondary sanctions do not merely influence individual decisions. They restructure systems. As banks exit relationships, entire sectors lose access to finance. Trade shifts to less transparent channels. Smaller institutions are crowded out. Concentration increases.

The motif binding this analysis is the shadow. Secondary sanctions cast a shadow far longer than their legal text, stretching into places never named.

A credible limitation must be addressed. Secondary sanctions are not omnipotent. Some states and institutions resist. China and Russia have invested in alternative payment systems. The EU has experimented with special purpose vehicles to facilitate trade outside US reach. Reconciling this requires honesty. Alternatives exist, but their scale and trust remain limited. For most actors, especially in smaller economies, resistance carries costs they cannot absorb.

Fear therefore remains rational.

The human dimension surfaces in the banker's reflections. He described feeling as though he had become an agent of a foreign policy he neither shaped nor endorsed. His staff absorbed the emotional fallout. Clients accused the bank of betrayal. Regulators demanded explanations. The bank complied outwardly and suffered inwardly.

Secondary sanctions blur accountability. Decisions appear private but are coerced. Harm appears incidental but is systemic. The issuing state can plausibly deny responsibility for outcomes it never formally mandated.

This ambiguity is strategic. It allows pressure to spread without negotiation. It also complicates correction. When damage occurs, there is no single policy to amend, only dispersed fear to recalibrate.

The shadow lengthens when secondary sanctions interact with compliance cultures described earlier in this book. Institutions already primed to over-comply interpret secondary risk expansively. Fear compounds fear.

The Malaysian banker noted that even after guidance softened, practices did not fully reverse. Relationships once exited were not rebuilt. The shadow persisted.

Resolve to a sharpened trade-off. Secondary sanctions are efficient precisely because they operate through fear rather than force. That efficiency delivers reach. It also exports collateral damage invisibly. The choice confronting sanctions architects is not whether fear works. It is whether they are willing to govern its consequences, or leave them to fall wherever the shadow lands.

Corporate strategists redefining risk

On 12 August 2020, in Rotterdam, the board of a European logistics multinational convened an emergency session after a brief alert from its legal team. Overnight, a senior US official had hinted at possible secondary sanctions linked to a regional port operator in which the company held a minority stake. No designation followed. No statute changed. Yet within forty-eight hours the firm suspended all expansion plans tied to that market. By October, it had announced a full withdrawal, writing off €180 million in projected investment and shuttering a facility that employed nearly eight hundred people along the coast.

The decision was not taken because the business had become illegal. It was taken because risk had been redefined.

Secondary sanctions exert their force not only through banks but through corporate strategy itself. The thesis of this section is that senior risk officers have become de facto translators of geopolitical pressure, redrawing corporate maps of opportunity and danger in ways that reverberate far beyond the balance sheet. When sanctions risk enters the boardroom, it rarely stays abstract. It reshapes where factories are built, which ports thrive, and which households retain a salary.

Observe the moment of reassessment. The Rotterdam firm had spent years cultivating the market. Demand forecasts were strong. Local partners were reliable. What changed was not the commercial logic, but the risk envelope. The legal team flagged potential exposure to US secondary sanctions. The compliance function modelled worst-case scenarios. The chief risk officer reframed the question: not whether the venture was profitable, but whether it could survive exclusion from dollar financing and US insurance markets.

Name the shift: sanctions risk internalisation. Explain that firms increasingly treat geopolitical signals as operational constraints rather than external noise. The consequence is strategic retreat even in the absence of formal prohibition.

The chief risk officer's presentation to the board was meticulous. Slides mapped revenue streams against currency exposure. Insurance dependencies were highlighted. A single slide showed the firm's reliance on US-based underwriters for maritime coverage. Another detailed the percentage of debt denominated in dollars. The message was implicit. One sanction-related shock could cascade across the enterprise.

Translate abstraction into decision. Expansion was paused. Capital expenditure frozen. Local contracts were allowed to lapse. Employees received notices framed in neutral language about "strategic realignment".

The ripple effects were immediate. Port throughput declined. Ancillary businesses lost orders. Families dependent on wages began to leave the area. The sanctions scare never materialised into law, but its economic footprint was real.

A second named example reinforces the pattern. In 2019, following increased enforcement actions under US sanctions programmes, a major Asian electronics manufacturer publicly announced it would cease sourcing components from a Middle Eastern supplier, despite no direct ban. In its annual report, the firm cited "heightened sanctions exposure" as a material risk. Subsequent analysis by trade economists noted a sharp contraction in the supplier's regional manufacturing cluster within six months.

Name the behaviour: pre-emptive de-risking. Explain that firms act on anticipated rather than actual constraints. The consequence is acceleration of economic disengagement.

Corporate strategists often justify these moves as prudence. They are correct within a narrow frame. Fiduciary duty demands avoidance of existential threats. Yet the aggregation of such decisions produces outcomes no single firm intends: hollowed markets, stranded workforces, and intensified dependency on fewer hubs.

The motif binding this section is the redraw. Risk officers redraw maps, quietly erasing regions from strategic plans.

Inside corporations, sanctions risk has migrated from legal footnote to central planning variable. Risk committees meet more frequently. Geopolitical monitoring becomes a standing agenda item. External counsel is consulted not for interpretation alone but for anticipation.

The Rotterdam firm's chief risk officer described the role candidly in a later industry forum. "We are not predicting policy," he said. "We are preparing for uncertainty." Preparation, in this context, meant withdrawal.

Metrics guide these judgements. Firms track exposure ratios: percentage of revenue linked to high-risk jurisdictions, share of financing reliant on sanctioning states, insurance concentration indices. These metrics, once obscure, now carry strategic weight.

Yet a credible limitation must be acknowledged. Not all firms retreat. Some double down, particularly those with limited exposure to sanctioning markets. Reconciling this requires nuance. Corporate responses vary by structure, geography, and ownership. State-backed enterprises often accept risks private firms cannot. Smaller firms sometimes operate below enforcement radar.

Still, for large multinationals embedded in global finance, the pattern is consistent. Fear compresses optionality.

The human consequences are often filtered out of boardroom models. The Rotterdam withdrawal included severance packages and transition assistance. It did not include a plan for the regional economy. That lay outside the firm's remit.

Employees experienced the decision as abrupt. Local managers struggled to explain a rationale that referenced distant regulators and hypothetical penalties. Trust eroded.

Secondary sanctions thus achieve leverage through multiplication. One signal prompts many withdrawals. Each withdrawal reinforces the perception of risk for others. The redraw accelerates.

Corporate strategists are aware of this dynamic. Some express discomfort. A risk officer at a multinational consumer goods firm described feeling like an "unpaid enforcement arm". Yet the logic of competition punishes hesitation. Firms that stay while others exit face concentrated scrutiny.

The redraw extends along supply chains. When anchor firms depart, suppliers follow or collapse. Port cities feel the contraction. Households adjust consumption. Migration increases.

These effects rarely appear in sanctions assessments. They emerge later, diffused and difficult to attribute.

The Rotterdam case also illustrates persistence. Two years after withdrawal, despite stabilisation of the geopolitical environment, the firm did not return. Capital, once redeployed, is slow to reverse. The redraw hardens.

This inertia matters. Secondary sanctions reshape economic geography not only temporarily but durably. Markets once deemed risky struggle to regain credibility.

The chief risk officer reflected privately that the firm had become more conservative across the board. The scare recalibrated risk appetite globally. Projects unrelated to sanctions were delayed. Fear generalised.

Resolve to a sharpened choice. Corporate strategists cannot ignore sanctions risk. Nor can they pretend their decisions are neutral. Each redraw carries distributive consequences. The question is whether firms will continue to treat sanctions exposure solely as a threat to be avoided, or as a factor to be weighed alongside responsibility for the worlds their strategies remake.

Allies, critics, and reluctant partners

On 3 October 2018, in Brussels, a senior official from a northern European finance ministry sat across a polished table from counterparts at the European Commission, rehearsing lines for a call with Washington. The immediate problem was narrow: how to respond to the latest US guidance on secondary sanctions tied to Iran. The political context was not. Opinion polls at home showed public anger at what newspapers framed as economic coercion. Exporters were lobbying furiously. Banks were already retreating. The datum that focused minds was simple and brutal: more than 70 per cent of the country's cross-border payments cleared through US-linked channels (European Central Bank, 2017). Allies feel pressure differently.

The negotiator's task was to reconcile alignment with autonomy. Formally, his government opposed the extraterritorial reach of the measures. Substantively, it could not afford to lose access to dollar markets. The paradox was visible to everyone in the room. They would protest, comply, and insist that both positions were consistent.

This section advances a clear thesis. Secondary sanctions strain alliances not by forcing open rupture, but by shifting power into informal spaces where consent blurs into acquiescence. Diplomats and officials in allied states become managers of dissonance, preserving ties while absorbing domestic anger, even as financial dependence quietly decides outcomes.

Observe the diplomatic choreography. Public statements reaffirm shared values and coordinated objectives. Private conversations are narrower, technical, and tense. Name this dynamic managed dissent. Explain that allies contest process rather than purpose, arguing about means while accepting ends. The consequence is an alliance that holds in form while fraying in practice.

The Brussels official's briefing notes were precise. He would emphasise the shared goal of non-proliferation. He would object to secondary sanctions as counterproductive. He would request clarity, timelines, and exemptions. He would not threaten retaliation. Threats would be ignored.

Translate abstraction into behaviour. The call ended with polite assurances. No policy changed. Within weeks, two domestic banks announced they would cease all Iran-related transactions, including those permitted under EU law. The finance ministry issued guidance urging proportionality. It was not followed.

A second named example sharpens the picture. In March 2022, following the expansion of sanctions related to Russia, a senior Japanese diplomat acknowledged publicly that certain secondary measures posed "challenges for alliance management" (Japan Ministry of Foreign Affairs, March 2022). Privately, officials worked to secure carve-outs for energy imports while signalling compliance to US counterparts. Domestic debate was heated. The outcome was compromise: reduced exposure without full disengagement.

Name the pattern: selective alignment. Explain that allies negotiate margins while accepting the centre. The consequence is uneven burden-sharing that leaves some domestic constituencies exposed and resentful.

The subtle motif binding this analysis is the fault line. Secondary sanctions open fault lines within alliances—between law and practice, rhetoric and reality, public anger and private dependency. The line is rarely visible at first. It widens over time.

Diplomats working along this fault line describe a distinctive professional strain. They are neither authors nor targets of the measures they must implement. They translate between capitals, regulators, and banks, each speaking a different language of obligation. Precision matters. So does tone.

In Brussels, the official's team drafted non-papers arguing that secondary sanctions undermined European sovereignty. They cited World Trade Organization principles and EU blocking statutes. They knew the arguments would not compel reversal. They hoped to shape interpretation.

Metrics intrude here as well. Treasury departments in allied states track exposure to sanctioning markets, mapping vulnerability by sector. When exposure is high, protest softens. When it is low, rhetoric hardens. Diplomacy follows balance sheets.

A credible limitation must be confronted. Alliances have endured secondary sanctions before. They endure now. Reconciling this requires acknowledging that shared security interests often outweigh economic grievances. Allies absorb costs to preserve broader cooperation. Yet endurance is not costless. Each episode deposits resentment.

The Brussels official noted that parliamentary hearings became more hostile after each sanctions round. Trust in alliance leadership eroded at the margins. Populist parties exploited the gap between declared sovereignty and lived dependence.

Secondary measures also alter intra-alliance hierarchies. States with less exposure gain moral clarity. Those with more exposure manage ambiguity. Over time, this asymmetry reshapes influence.

The fault line appears again in legal practice. Domestic courts in allied states sometimes uphold blocking statutes. Firms ignore them. Governments rarely enforce. Law yields to fear.

The negotiator's most difficult task was domestic explanation. He could not admit dependence without undermining political authority. He could not deny it without losing credibility. He spoke of "complex trade-offs". Voters heard evasion.

These dynamics do not require bad faith. They arise from structure. Secondary sanctions centralise power without formalising governance. Allies are left to improvise.

The long-term implication is subtle but significant. When alliances rely on coercive spillovers rather than negotiated consent, cohesion becomes procedural rather than emotional. Cooperation persists. Confidence thins.

Return to the motif. Fault lines can remain dormant. They can also slip.

Resolve to a sharpened choice. Allies confronting secondary sanctions face a test not of loyalty, but of agency. They can continue to manage dissent quietly, preserving access while absorbing anger, or they can invest in collective mechanisms that align power with consent. The measures will strain alliances either way. The question is whether the strain is acknowledged and governed, or merely endured until the fault line gives way.

The view from sanctioned societies

In March 2016, in Beirut, a mid-level official from a European foreign ministry sat in a cramped office above a pharmacy listening to a paediatrician explain why antibiotics had become intermittent. The doctor did not mention sanctions. He talked about distributors who no longer answered calls, banks that returned transfers without explanation, and suppliers who demanded cash in advance. The official wrote notes anyway. Later that evening, in his hotel room, he reread a letter sent months earlier to his department by a hospital director in the same city. The phrasing matched. So did the silence.

Models do not write letters.

This section advances a simple but disruptive thesis. First-hand testimony from sanctioned societies, when encountered directly by sanctions architects, unsettles abstract policy models and can provoke genuine reconsideration of tactics. Not always. Not enough. But sometimes decisively.

Observe the architecture of sanctions design. Analysts work with indicators: trade volumes, inflation rates, currency movements, political concessions. Civilian impact appears as a variable to be mitigated, often through exemptions. Name the problem: representational distance. Explain that distance allows harm to be acknowledged without being felt. The consequence is confidence in models that capture pressure but miss texture.

The Beirut visit was not planned as a listening exercise. It was meant to assess compliance with humanitarian exemptions. The official expected to confirm that carve-outs functioned adequately. Instead, he encountered a pattern. Payments delayed. Shipments rerouted. Costs rising invisibly.

Translate abstraction into experience. A shipment of insulin arrives weeks late because an intermediary bank flags the transaction. The exemption exists. The practice fails.

The official returned home with transcripts and photographs. He also carried unease. The data he had trusted did not account for what he had seen.

A second named example illustrates the effect more starkly. In 2019, a small delegation from the United Nations Office for the Coordination of Humanitarian Affairs travelled to Caracas to assess sanctions impact. According to internal summaries later cited in academic reviews, staff were struck by the discrepancy between reported humanitarian flows and conditions on the ground. Aid volumes had not collapsed. Access had.

Name the insight: friction matters. Explain that sanctions operate not only by restricting goods, but by multiplying transaction costs and uncertainty. The consequence is attrition rather than blockade.

The motif binding this section is the letter. Letters arrive where models do not. They carry names, dates, and handwriting. They demand attention.

Sanctions architects encounter these voices unevenly. Some travel. Some read. Some delegate the task. The effect depends on proximity. Those who listen closely often describe a shift in how they understand responsibility.

In Beirut, the official requested follow-up meetings. He asked to see bank correspondence. He spoke with importers. Patterns emerged. Exemptions were interpreted narrowly by banks fearing penalties. Local institutions bore the cost.

The letters he later reviewed were not accusatory. They were explanatory. "We comply with all guidance," one read. "Yet funds do not arrive."

Translate this into policy tension. Sanctions design assumes rational compliance. Sanctions practice is shaped by fear.

The official presented his findings internally. The reception was mixed. Colleagues acknowledged the issues. Some questioned representativeness. Others worried about precedent. Still, a small change followed. Guidance language was clarified. Outreach to banks increased. The adjustment was incremental. It mattered locally.

A credible limitation must be stated. First-hand testimony does not always change policy. Sometimes it is absorbed, filed, and forgotten.

Reconciling this requires honesty. Institutions have inertia. Strategic priorities dominate. Voices from sanctioned societies compete with security imperatives.

Yet the effect is not zero.

A third example comes from correspondence. In 2020, sanctions officials in Washington received a coordinated set of letters from diaspora organisations describing the impact of banking exits on remittances. According to a Treasury Department review later discussed in a policy journal, the volume and specificity of the submissions prompted an internal reassessment of general licences related to personal remittances. The rules did not dissolve. They shifted at the margins.

Name the mechanism: moral feedback. Explain that testimony introduces ethical salience into technical systems. The consequence is recalibration rather than reversal.

The letter motif returns here. Unlike metrics, letters persist. They can be reread. They circulate informally. They haunt.

Sanctions architects who have travelled to sanctioned societies often describe a lingering effect. One official recalled thinking differently about "over-compliance" after watching a local NGO attempt, and fail, to pay staff salaries. The exemption existed. The bank refused.

Translate abstraction into time. Weeks pass. Salaries lapse. Staff leave. Programmes shrink. None of this appears immediately in macro data.

Listening also exposes uneven impact. Sanctions rarely affect societies uniformly. Elites adapt. Informal networks expand. Middle layers suffer attrition. Letters often come from these layers: professionals, small business owners, teachers.

This challenges a common assumption. Pressure does not always rise evenly. It pools.

The Beirut official later advocated for integrating field testimony into sanctions review cycles. The proposal was modest: a standing requirement that humanitarian impact assessments include qualitative inputs from affected communities. It was accepted on a pilot basis.

Metrics alone had proven insufficient.

The motif surfaces again in resistance. Some colleagues worried that listening would weaken resolve. Others argued the opposite: that blind pressure eroded legitimacy. The debate was quiet but real.

The sanctioned societies themselves are not passive. They adapt, circumvent, endure. Their letters often describe ingenuity alongside hardship. This complicates narratives of victimhood. It also complicates design.

A final example underscores this. During a 2021 visit to a Central Asian state under sectoral sanctions, an EU official met entrepreneurs who had reorganised supply chains through third countries. They asked not for relief, but for clarity. Uncertainty was their greatest cost.

Name the request: predictability. Explain that sanctions design often prioritises flexibility for issuers over predictability for subjects. The consequence is excessive risk aversion by intermediaries.

The official reported that meeting changed how he read compliance statistics. High compliance no longer signalled success. It signalled fear.

Return to the letter. Back in Beirut, months after the visit, the paediatrician sent an update. Antibiotic supplies had stabilised. A local bank had resumed limited processing after new guidance. The change was fragile. It was also real.

Resolve to a sharpened choice. Sanctions architects can continue to rely primarily on models that abstract away lived experience, adjusting only when harm becomes politically visible. Or they can institutionalise listening, treating testimony not as anecdote but as data of a different kind. Letters will arrive either way. The question is whether anyone will read them closely enough to let them reshape the system that made them necessary.

Chapter 8
Counting Outcomes And Blowback

On a grey morning in February 2015, a policy analyst sat in a windowless office in Washington staring at a spreadsheet that refused to cohere. The rows were tidy enough: inflation, exchange rates, export volumes, approval ratings. The columns were dated meticulously, month by month. What the sheet would not do was tell a story. The sanctions regime under review had been in place for three years. The economy it targeted was clearly strained. And yet the political concessions that had justified the measures remained elusive. The analyst circled one figure in red, then crossed it out. Correlation was easy. Causation was not.

Success, it turned out, was harder to count than pressure.

Sanctions are imposed with objectives. They are defended with metrics. They are sustained through narratives of effectiveness. Yet when examined closely, the question of whether sanctions "work" often dissolves into argument about what, exactly, working means. Is success economic pain, behavioural change, political signalling, deterrence of others, or simply the absence of better tools? This chapter enters that uncertainty, not to resolve it neatly, but to show how outcomes are constructed, contested, and sometimes quietly ignored.

The modern sanctions regime is obsessed with measurement. Dashboards proliferate. Indicators are tracked. Reviews are scheduled. The language of evaluation has become fluent. What has not kept pace is agreement on meaning. The analyst in Washington knew this. His task was to brief senior officials ahead of a renewal decision. He needed to say whether the sanctions were effective. He also knew that effectiveness depended on assumptions no spreadsheet could verify.

This chapter follows those assumptions as they are made, defended, and revised. It traces how sanctions architects define success, how they grapple with unintended consequences, how they interpret failure, and how some attempt—often against institutional resistance—to build feedback loops capable of learning rather than merely justifying.

The first problem is definitional. Sanctions are rarely imposed with a single, testable goal. Official objectives often combine pressure, signalling, and deterrence. Private objectives diverge further. Some actors hope for regime change. Others for negotiation. Still others for containment. The analyst's spreadsheet could show economic distress. It could not tell him which political outcome that distress should produce, or on what timetable.

This ambiguity is not accidental. It creates flexibility. It also creates fragility. Claims of success can be asserted early and defended indefinitely, even as outcomes drift.

From this ambiguity flows the second challenge: blowback. Sanctions do not operate in closed systems. They redirect trade, capital, and influence across a densely interconnected world. A researcher mapping trade flows notices that exports do not disappear; they reroute. Industries in third countries expand unexpectedly. Political alignments shift. Pressure intended for one target diffuses outward, sometimes stabilising rivals, sometimes undermining allies.

These effects are often described as unintended. The researcher in this chapter resists that framing. He argues instead that they are under-analysed. When sanctions reshape global patterns, they produce winners as well as losers. Those outcomes feed back into geopolitics, often in ways that complicate the original strategy.

The chapter then turns to failure, the most uncomfortable subject in sanctions policy. Some campaigns do not achieve their stated aims. They harden regimes. They entrench elites. They exhaust diplomatic capital. Inside institutions, these failures are rarely labelled as such. They are reframed as incomplete, premature, or obstructed by external factors. Post-mortems, when they occur, are often defensive.

Yet failure can be instructive. Insiders who have lived through unsuccessful campaigns sometimes become the most persuasive advocates for redesign rather than abandonment. They argue not that sanctions should disappear, but that they should change: narrower targets, clearer objectives, better integration with diplomacy, and more honest evaluation.

Learning, however, requires feedback. And feedback requires systems capable of hearing inconvenient signals. This is where innovation enters the story. A cross-functional team attempts to integrate humanitarian data, banking reports, and trade flows into a single review process. The effort is messy. Data arrives late and incomplete. Interpretations clash. Still, the experiment reveals something crucial: outcomes look different when viewed from multiple angles at once.

The analyst in Washington would have welcomed such a system. Instead, he worked with partial views. He knew that inflation spikes might reflect global commodity cycles as much as sanctions. He knew that currency movements could be driven by domestic mismanagement. He also knew that political concessions, when they came, might owe more to internal dynamics than external pressure. The spreadsheet could not adjudicate these possibilities. It could only present them side by side.

A subtle motif runs through this chapter: the echo. Sanctions send signals outward. Outcomes echo back, altered by distance and interference. Some echoes are loud—currency crashes, trade collapses. Others are faint—gradual political shifts, quiet humanitarian strain. Counting outcomes requires deciding which echoes matter.

This decision is not neutral. It reflects institutional incentives. Agencies responsible for sanctions are often tasked with defending them. Metrics that confirm effectiveness travel upward more easily than those that complicate the story. Blowback is noted, but rarely foregrounded. Learning competes with legitimacy.

The modern relevance is stark. As sanctions are deployed more frequently and more expansively, the question of how to judge them grows more urgent. Public debates oscillate between triumphalism and scepticism, often without shared criteria. Policymakers renew measures citing success that is asserted rather than demonstrated. Critics cite harm without tracing causality. Both sides talk past each other.

This chapter does not offer a definitive metric of success. It offers something more useful: an anatomy of how success and failure are constructed inside the system. It shows how economic indicators become proxies for political change, how unintended effects are discounted or deferred, how failure is reframed to preserve authority, and how feedback loops struggle to gain traction in institutions built for control rather than adaptation.

By the end of the chapter, the analyst's spreadsheet returns, but altered. It is no longer a tool for verdicts. It becomes a prompt for questions. What would count as success here? For whom? Over what horizon? At what cost elsewhere?

Those questions do not weaken sanctions. They discipline them. The chapters that follow will take up that discipline, asking how pressure might be redesigned without blindness, and how architects might learn to listen not only for the loud echoes of pain, but for the quieter signals that tell them whether the system they built is doing what they claim.

What counts as success

On 14 January 2016, in Washington, a policy analyst at the US Treasury's Office of Foreign Assets Control opened a briefing file marked "Renewal Assessment". The sanctions regime under review had been in place for almost four years. The economic data were unambiguous. Inflation in the target country had breached 40 per cent. The currency had lost more than half its value since 2012 (International Monetary Fund, 2015). Export revenues were sharply down. What the file could not say was whether any of this had delivered the political concessions promised when the measures were announced.

Pressure was visible. Success was not.

The analyst's task was to advise senior officials on whether the regime was "working". That single word carried more ambiguity than any figure on the page. He could point to macroeconomic distress. He could cite business exits and capital flight. He could not, with confidence, trace a straight line from those outcomes to the political behaviour the sanctions were meant to change.

This section advances a precise thesis. Claims of sanctions success are fragile because they depend on contested definitions, selective metrics, and interpretive leaps across systems crowded with intervening variables. Success is not measured; it is constructed.

Observe the analyst's first problem. Sanctions are imposed with stated objectives, yet those objectives are often plural and elastic. Official documents speak of "changing behaviour", "imposing costs", "signalling resolve", and "deterring others". Each implies a different metric. Name this multiplicity goal dispersion. Explain that when goals multiply, almost any outcome can be framed as partial success. The consequence is resilience of policy narratives even in the absence of clear causal proof.

The analyst began by listing indicators commonly used to demonstrate effectiveness. Exchange rate depreciation. GDP contraction. Declining foreign direct investment. These were familiar. They were also indirect. None constituted political behaviour. They were proxies.

Translate abstraction into method. He attempted to correlate economic stress with observable political concessions: changes in negotiating posture, legislative amendments, shifts in foreign policy alignment. The correlations were weak. Timing did not align. Some concessions preceded economic collapse. Others followed unrelated diplomatic developments.

The five-word sentence came to him unbidden. *Pressure is not persuasion.*

Name the distinction. Sanctions reliably generate pressure. They do not reliably generate compliance. Explain that political systems mediate economic pain unevenly. Elites shield themselves. Narratives of resistance mobilise support. The consequence is decoupling between economic indicators and political outcomes.

A first named example illustrates the difficulty. Following the imposition of comprehensive sanctions on Iran in the early 2010s, US officials frequently cited falling oil exports and currency depreciation as evidence of success. Yet scholarly analyses later noted that the decisive factor leading to negotiations in 2013 was a complex interaction of electoral change, internal elite bargaining, and diplomatic signalling, not economic distress alone (Maloney, *Brookings*, 2015). Sanctions mattered. They were not sufficient.

The analyst knew this literature. He also knew how selectively it was invoked.

The second named example complicates matters further. After the introduction of sectoral sanctions against Russia in 2014, European policymakers pointed to slowed growth and capital outflows as validation. Subsequent studies by the European Bank for Reconstruction and Development, however, found that a significant portion of the economic downturn reflected oil price shocks rather than sanctions effects (EBRD, 2016). Attribution blurred. Success claims persisted.

Name the practice: attribution stretch. Explain that when multiple shocks coincide, sanctions are credited for outcomes they did not solely cause. The consequence is overconfidence in tool efficacy.

The analyst faced this problem daily. His briefing required judgement. Numbers alone would not decide. He had to choose which indicators to emphasise and which caveats to include. He knew which choice would travel further up the hierarchy.

The subtle motif threading this section is the ledger. Sanctions success is imagined as a balance sheet: costs imposed versus concessions gained. The problem is that entries on each side are denominated differently.

On the cost side sit quantifiable metrics. Inflation rates. Revenue losses. Trade contraction. On the concessions side sit qualitative judgements. Tone shifts. Partial agreements. Silence. The ledger never balances cleanly.

The analyst attempted a different approach. He traced specific policy demands made at the outset of the sanctions and assessed progress against each. Some demands had softened. Others remained unmet. New demands had been added. The goalposts moved.

Name the phenomenon: objective drift. Explain that as time passes, sanctions objectives evolve, often in response to domestic politics rather than target behaviour. The consequence is retrospective success claims untethered from original aims.

A credible limitation must be acknowledged. Some sanctions do achieve clear, observable goals. Asset freezes that block specific transactions. Export controls that halt particular technologies. Reconciling this requires distinction. Tactical success does not equal strategic success. The analyst accepted this. His problem lay with the latter.

He also confronted deterrence, the most elusive claim of all. Officials argued that sanctions deter others from similar behaviour. The analyst asked how such deterrence could be observed. Absence of action is ambiguous. It may reflect unrelated calculations. Deterrence is inferred, not measured.

The ledger motif returns here. Deterrence entries are speculative credits. They pad the success column without verification.

The analyst's briefing draft grew cautious. He wrote that sanctions had "contributed to economic pressure" and "shaped the negotiating environment". He avoided causal absolutes. His supervisor struck out qualifiers. The final version spoke of "demonstrated effectiveness".

Translate this into institutional behaviour. Success narratives are simplified as they rise. Ambiguity thins. By the time it reaches public statements, effectiveness is asserted rather than argued.

This process has consequences. It conditions future design. If sanctions are deemed successful on thin evidence, they are more likely to be reused. Tool reliance deepens.

The analyst later reflected that the most honest metric he had was uncertainty. He could not say the sanctions failed. He could not say they succeeded. He could say they imposed costs and created leverage that other factors converted, partially, into outcomes.

The ledger still would not close.

The motif appears again when considering time horizons. Short-term pain is visible. Long-term political change is slow. Sanctions are often judged before effects can plausibly materialise. Renewal cycles incentivise premature verdicts.

What counts as success then becomes procedural. Did the sanctions remain in place? Were they enforced? Did allies comply? Process substitutes for outcome.

Resolve to a sharpened choice. Sanctions architects can continue to treat economic distress as a stand-in for political achievement, filling ledgers with costs while inferring concessions. Or they can accept uncertainty as a core feature, designing measures with clearer objectives, explicit assumptions, and humility about attribution. Success will remain contested either way. The difference lies in whether that contest is acknowledged openly, or settled quietly by those with the pen.

Unintended economic and political effects

In October 2017, in Tbilisi, a trade economist opened a customs database and noticed something that did not fit. Exports of rebar and industrial fasteners from Georgia to a small Central Asian state had tripled in eighteen months. The volumes were too large for domestic demand. The prices were oddly consistent. When the economist overlaid shipping data, a pattern emerged: onward movement to a sanctioned market through two intermediaries. The date mattered. The spike began weeks after a new sanctions package was announced elsewhere. The place mattered too. Georgia was not a target. It had become a corridor.

Trade does not vanish. It reroutes.

The thesis of this section is plain. Sanctions generate unintended economic and political effects because they operate within dense, adaptive systems. Pressure applied at one node redistributes activity across others, often strengthening actors and pathways policymakers did not anticipate. Ignoring this interdependence does not eliminate blowback; it obscures it.

Observe the economist's method. He compared pre- and post-sanctions trade flows across similar commodities, controlling for price and transport costs. He then traced firm-level ownership and shipping routes. The results were consistent. Where direct trade contracted, indirect trade expanded. Name the phenomenon: displacement. Explain that sanctions shift commerce rather than extinguish it. The consequence is the creation of new intermediaries and rents.

The five-word sentence came easily. *Markets find new paths.*

The Georgian case was not unique. A second named example illustrates the scale. After the imposition of sectoral sanctions on Russia in 2014, several studies documented sharp increases in EU exports of certain machinery components to Kazakhstan and Armenia, followed by corresponding rises in Russian imports from those states (Crozet and Hinz, *Economic Policy*, 2016). The goods were legal in transit. Their destination was not concealed. The pathway was.

Translate abstraction into behaviour. Firms reconfigure supply chains. Logistics companies specialise in triangulation. Customs authorities struggle to distinguish growth from diversion. None of this violates sanctions law directly. It exploits its seams.

The economist presented his findings to a regional development ministry. Officials were ambivalent. Export growth looked good in headline figures. Jobs followed. Political leaders welcomed diversification. The fact that growth depended on sanctions elsewhere was awkward.

Name the tension: perverse benefit. Explain that third countries can gain economically from others' isolation. The consequence is misaligned incentives that complicate coalition enforcement.

Blowback extends beyond trade. Financial flows adapt similarly. When banks in sanctioning jurisdictions exit relationships, smaller institutions in permissive environments step in. Risk concentrates. Oversight thins. The economist mapped correspondent banking links and found that a handful of mid-sized banks had become pivotal conduits. Their balance sheets grew rapidly. So did their political influence.

Translate this into political effect. Governments hosting these intermediaries become stakeholders in continuation. Their diplomats resist measures that threaten newfound revenue. Alignment frays.

The motif binding this analysis is the current. Sanctions push against a current of global interdependence. When the force increases, the current bends around it, sometimes eroding banks far from the original site.

The economist's work expanded to energy markets. Following restrictions on certain crude exports, shipping data revealed longer routes, ship-to-ship transfers, and increased insurance premiums. Costs rose. Revenues did not collapse. The added margins accrued to traders and logistics firms adept at opacity.

Name the effect: rent creation. Explain that complexity generates profits for those who navigate it. The consequence is the entrenchment of actors with an interest in persistence.

Political systems feel the current as well. In some third countries, sudden trade booms strain regulatory capacity. Corruption risks increase. Opposition parties accuse governments of complicity. Public trust erodes.

A third named example underscores this dynamic. In 2019, investigative journalists in a Balkan state reported on a surge in exports of chemical precursors to a sanctioned market via shell companies. Parliamentary inquiries followed. The government denied wrongdoing. The issue destabilised a fragile coalition. Sanctions elsewhere had altered domestic politics here.

A credible limitation must be addressed. Not all displacement is harmful. Some rerouting mitigates civilian impact by sustaining supply. Reconciling this requires discrimination. The problem is not movement per se, but unmanaged movement that empowers opaque actors and undermines governance.

The economist argued for this nuance. He did not claim sanctions were futile. He claimed they were incomplete analyses of systems. His recommendation was simple: integrate third-country effects into design and review.

Metrics make this possible. Trade anomaly indices. Network centrality measures for intermediaries. Insurance premium spreads. When tracked, blowback becomes visible.

Yet institutions resist. Accounting for interdependence complicates success narratives. It demands coordination across agencies and borders. It exposes trade-offs.

The current motif returns when sanctions evolve. As measures tighten, currents intensify. New corridors open. Old ones close. The system never rests.

The economist's most unsettling finding concerned political feedback. In several third countries benefiting from rerouted trade, public opinion shifted subtly against sanctioning states perceived as destabilising. Soft power eroded. Alliances thinned at the margins.

Translate this into strategic cost. Sanctions may weaken targets while strengthening alternative blocs and intermediaries. The ledger fills on one side and empties on another.

The economist presented his work at a closed-door workshop. Some officials welcomed it. Others worried it would "undermine resolve". The response illustrated the central dilemma. Understanding blowback does not require abandoning sanctions. It requires governing them.

Resolve to a sharpened choice. Sanctions architects can continue to treat unintended effects as regrettable noise, correcting only when scandals erupt. Or they can design with currents in mind, anticipating displacement, monitoring intermediaries, and adjusting before rents harden into interests. Global interdependence will not disappear. The question is whether sanctions policy will finally account for it, or continue to be surprised by the routes commerce takes when pressure rises.

Learning from failed sanctions campaigns

In December 2018, in a windowless conference room in Washington, a review team projected a single figure onto the wall: a 4.2 per cent contraction. It was the estimated GDP decline attributed to a multi-year sanctions regime, drawn from an inter-agency assessment circulated after months of delay. The number was precise. The mood was not. The target government remained in place. None of the stated political concessions had materialised. The date mattered because the sanctions had been escalated in 2012. The place mattered because this was where success had been declared, repeatedly, in public.

The paradox was immediate. Economic pain had been real. Political effect had been absent.

This section advances a clear thesis. Failed sanctions campaigns are not anomalies to be buried but laboratories to be studied. Where post-mortems are honest, they refine tools and sharpen judgement. Where institutions defend narratives, learning stalls and mistakes recur.

Observe how failure is usually recognised. Rarely does a campaign end with a formal admission. Instead, goals quietly shift. Timelines extend. New measures are layered on top of old ones. Name this behaviour: narrative drift. Explain that institutions struggle to concede that pressure has not translated into leverage. The consequence is accumulation without recalibration.

The first named example is well documented. Comprehensive sanctions against Iraq in the 1990s devastated civilian welfare while entrenching regime control. Multiple UN reports, including the Oil-for-Food Programme inquiries (UN, 2005), detailed diversion, corruption, and limited political impact. Insiders involved in later reforms drew a stark lesson: broad embargoes produced humanitarian catastrophe without delivering compliance.

Translate this abstraction into institutional change. The experience informed the shift towards targeted sanctions in the early 2000s. Asset freezes and travel bans replaced blanket trade restrictions. This was learning. It came late, but it came.

A second example shows how learning can falter. Sanctions imposed on Iran between 2010 and 2015 are often cited as a success because they preceded the Joint Comprehensive Plan of Action. Yet internal assessments revealed disagreement about causality. Economic pressure mattered. So did diplomacy, regional security calculations, and electoral change within Iran. When the agreement later collapsed, some officials argued the sanctions had never addressed core incentives. Others insisted pressure simply needed more time.

Name the dispute: attribution conflict. Explain that when multiple variables drive outcomes, institutions select the story that preserves their role. The consequence is contested memory rather than shared learning.

Inside these debates were analysts pushing for redesign rather than abandonment. One policy adviser, interviewed years later, described drafting a memo titled *What we missed.* It catalogued assumptions that proved false: that economic elites would fracture, that public hardship would translate into political pressure, that enforcement capacity would scale indefinitely. The memo circulated briefly. It was never formally endorsed.

Five words captured the moment. *Failure rarely signs its name.*

The motif binding this section is the autopsy. Post-mortems reveal causes only if the body is examined honestly. Cosmetic reports tell comforting stories. Diagnostic ones unsettle careers.

Translate the process. A genuine sanctions autopsy asks specific questions. Which behaviours changed? Which adapted? Which actors gained power? What signals were misread? These are observable metrics: changes in elite cohesion, emergence of new trade intermediaries, shifts in public opinion measured by credible surveys, enforcement costs over time.

In several campaigns, these questions were not asked. Or when asked, answers were ignored.

A credible limitation must be acknowledged. Some sanctions fail because targets are unusually resilient or insulated. Learning cannot overcome all structural constraints. Reconciling this means distinguishing between intrinsic limits and design flaws. Many failures involve both.

Consider the case of long-standing sanctions on Cuba. Decades of economic restriction did not produce regime change. Internal US reviews, including academic analyses by Hufbauer et al. (Peterson Institute, 2009), concluded that the measures entrenched nationalist narratives and provided a convenient external scapegoat. Insiders later argued for engagement. Institutional inertia prevailed.

Observe the pattern. Where failure threatens identity, institutions defend the tool rather than interrogate its use. Name this dynamic:

tool loyalty. Explain that sanctions become symbols of resolve. The consequence is resistance to evidence.

Learning does occur at the margins. Some enforcement agencies now commission independent evaluations. Some treasuries invite humanitarian organisations to review impacts. These practices remain uneven.

The insiders who push hardest for learning often do so quietly. They frame critiques as technical adjustments rather than strategic reversals. They speak of thresholds, sequencing, exemptions. This is survival. It is also partial reform.

The autopsy motif returns in a different form. Without shared findings, each new campaign repeats old mistakes under new names. Over-compliance reappears. Displacement is rediscovered. Humanitarian harm is acknowledged after the fact.

Translate this into cost. Failed learning wastes political capital, harms civilians, and dulls leverage. It also undermines credibility with allies asked to enforce measures whose efficacy is asserted, not demonstrated.

Resolve to a sharpened choice. Sanctions architects can institutionalise failure analysis, building mandatory post-mortems with protected dissent and external scrutiny. Or they can continue to rely on narratives of resolve, accepting repetition as the price of certainty. The tools will not disappear. The question is whether institutions will finally learn from their own autopsies, or keep closing the report before the cause of death is written.

Building better feedback loops

On 17 May 2021, in Brussels, a dashboard flickered to life on a secure screen inside the European External Action Service. It showed three lines moving in different directions: humanitarian shipment approvals, cross-border trade volumes, and correspondent banking rejections. The data came from three organisations that rarely shared rooms, let alone systems: a UN humanitarian cluster, a customs analytics unit, and a consortium of European banks. The paradox was blunt. Sanctions were tightening. Civilian harm was rising. Yet leverage was flat.

Someone had to connect the lines.

This section advances a clear thesis. Sanctions that learn in real time outperform sanctions that merely persist. Feedback loops—designed, resourced, and protected—can reduce unintended harm while preserving pressure. Where they are absent, policy drifts; where they exist, design adapts.

Five words set the problem. *Pressure without feedback misleads.*

Observe the initial condition. Sanctions are launched with goals and assumptions. They enter complex systems—markets, logistics, social networks—whose responses are dynamic. Name the failure mode: static governance. Explain that when measures do not ingest evidence as they operate, designers infer success from activity rather than effect. The consequence is escalation untethered from outcomes.

The Brussels dashboard emerged from frustration with that pattern. A cross-functional team—policy officers, humanitarian analysts, trade economists, and compliance specialists—argued that the system could be made legible while it ran. Their proposition was simple: integrate signals already being produced and review them on a fixed cadence with authority to adjust.

Translate the abstraction. The team pooled three datasets. First, humanitarian data: licence approvals, delivery times, stockouts, and incident reports from field partners, updated weekly. Second, trade flows: customs declarations, shipping manifests, and mirror statistics to detect rerouting, updated monthly. Third, banking reports: volumes of rejected payments, de-risking decisions, and escalation notes from compliance desks, updated fortnightly. None of this required new law. It required permission.

Name the architecture: the adaptive review loop. Explain that it differs from after-action reviews by operating during the campaign. The consequence was immediate. Within two review cycles, the team identified a choke point unrelated to targets: an ambiguous exemption phrase that banks interpreted conservatively. A clarification letter—two paragraphs—restored shipments of insulin and dialysis supplies within weeks, according to UN OCHA reporting (2021).

A second named example shows the model travelling. In 2019, the US Treasury's Office of Foreign Assets Control piloted a sanctions review process incorporating bank feedback and humanitarian indicators for a limited regime. Internal guidance encouraged analysts to flag "non-target harm" signals alongside evasion indicators (OFAC, 2019). The experiment did not soften enforcement. It sharpened it. Resources shifted towards nodes showing adaptive behaviour, while licences were streamlined where harm outpaced leverage.

Observe the behaviour change. Analysts stopped arguing about intent and started discussing metrics. Name the shift: evidentiary discipline. Explain that when feedback is institutionalised, debate moves from ideology to calibration. The consequence is fewer blunt instruments.

The motif binding this section is the thermostat. A system with a thermostat senses temperature and adjusts heat. Without one, rooms overheat while occupants argue about whether the boiler works. The thermostat appears again when the team expanded its inputs.

Translate the next layer. Trade rerouting is not a moral failure; it is a signal. When sanctioned goods detour through third countries, the question is not whether to condemn the detour but whether the control point sits in the wrong place. By overlaying customs anomalies with banking data, the team identified a small number of freight forwarders acting as multipliers. Targeted designations followed. Blanket restrictions did not.

Metrics mattered. The team tracked changes in average delivery times for humanitarian cargo, variance in trade flows for controlled items, and the ratio of false-positive bank rejections to confirmed evasion cases. These are observable behaviours, not abstractions. They changed.

A credible limitation must be faced. Feedback loops can be gamed. Targets adapt to signals. Reconciling this requires designing loops that distinguish between noise and manipulation. The team addressed the risk by separating operational data from policy signals and rotating indicators. Transparency to partners did not mean predictability to evaders.

A second limitation concerns politics. Adaptive systems appear indecisive. Leaders prefer certainty. The Brussels team survived because its mandate was narrow and its authority clear. Scaling the model requires political cover.

The thermostat motif returns. When rooms cool too quickly, occupants complain. When heat rises unchecked, pipes burst. The art lies in adjustment, not stasis.

Translate the human dimension. Bank compliance officers, previously isolated, became data contributors. Their escalation notes—patterns of fear-driven de-risking, bottlenecks in correspondent chains—entered policy discussions. In return, guidance became clearer. This reciprocity reduced over-compliance without weakening enforcement.

Evidence supports the approach. Studies on adaptive regulation show improved outcomes where feedback is timely and authority to adjust is real (Ayres and Braithwaite, 1992). In sanctions contexts, early pilots suggest similar gains, though the literature remains thin.

Resolve to a sharpened choice. Sanctions architects can build thermostats into their systems—integrating humanitarian data, trade flows, and banking signals with authority to act—or they can continue to read the temperature after the pipes have burst. Adaptive architectures demand humility and discipline. They also offer something rare in economic statecraft: the chance to learn while acting, and to preserve leverage without pretending that persistence alone equals success.

Chapter 9
Doubters, Whistleblowers, And Exits

On a grey morning in October 2018, in a government building a short walk from Whitehall, a senior sanctions lawyer printed a draft designation and reached for a pencil. The document was clean, internally consistent, and almost certain to pass review. In the margin beside a clause on "reasonably foreseeable effects", she wrote a small question mark, then circled it. No one else would see it. The pencil left no audit trail. Still, the mark lingered.

Careers in sanctions rarely begin with doubt. They begin with competence: mastering statutes, learning lists, calibrating risk. For years, the work rewards precision and stamina. It offers proximity to power without spectacle. The paradox that animates this chapter is that the same systems that prize technical excellence are also remarkably good at absorbing unease. Doubt accumulates quietly, often invisibly, inside people who are otherwise succeeding.

This chapter enters that interior space. Not to romanticise dissent, nor to stage a morality play, but to understand what happens when architects of financial pressure begin to question the justice or efficacy of the structures they maintain. The focus is not on scandals but on sediment: the slow layering of misgivings that reshape behaviour long before they surface as exits, reforms, or silence.

The modern sanctions regime depends on discretion. Every chapter so far has shown how much judgement sits between policy and effect. Here, that judgement turns inward. The question is no longer only what pressure does to targets, but what it does to those who apply it.

Consider the drafter with the pencil. Her doubts did not arrive as a single revelation. They arrived through repetition. A licence delayed for lack of clarity. A humanitarian exemption narrowed by risk aversion. A briefing note that spoke of "manageable impact" while field reports suggested otherwise. Each instance was defensible. Together, they created friction. Cognitive dissonance is the name given to this condition, but the term is too tidy. In practice, it feels like static.

The book has followed sanctions architects across offices and institutions. This chapter follows them across thresholds. The first threshold is internal. Insiders begin to annotate doubts not because they reject the tool, but because they see its limits more clearly than those outside. Technical success sharpens moral perception. The better one understands the machine, the harder it becomes to pretend it runs itself.

Doubt takes different forms. For some, it is empirical: measures do not produce the promised concessions. For others, it is distributive: harms fall where leverage is thin. For a few, it is temporal: pressure persists long after its rationale has faded. What unites these strands is the absence of obvious outlets. Institutions are designed to channel risk, not remorse.

The next threshold is choice. Speaking out is neither binary nor heroic by default. Whistleblowing law imagines a clear path from knowledge to disclosure. Reality offers a thicket of partial options: internal reports that stall, conversations that change tone, memos that are rewritten until their edge dulls. Silence, too, is active. It preserves careers and relationships while extracting a private cost.

One data analyst, working in a financial intelligence unit in 2020, faced such a choice. He had built models tracing trade diversion and could see that a set of secondary measures was rerouting commerce without increasing pressure on decision-makers. His findings circulated. They were acknowledged. Then they were bracketed by urgency. When a journalist contacted him months later, he declined. Within the year, he resigned. No leak followed. No inquiry opened. Yet his departure mattered. Expertise left the room.

This pattern recurs. Many moral doubts never become external scandals. They become attrition. The system adjusts not through rupture but through thinning. Analysts who leave take with them not only skill but memory. Institutions notice the gap only when it widens.

Not all doubters exit. Some stay and reform from within. Their scepticism is procedural rather than oppositional. A compliance chief in a European bank, appointed after a bruising enforcement action, used his credibility to argue for narrower designations and clearer humanitarian guidance. He did not challenge the legitimacy of sanctions. He challenged their execution. By insisting on better definitions and documented rationales, he reduced over-compliance while strengthening defensibility. His influence did not soften pressure; it focused it.

These internal reformers complicate the story. They show that scepticism can coexist with loyalty, and that institutions are not monoliths. Culture matters. Training matters. So does the ability to speak without being marked as unreliable. The line between constructive dissent and career risk is thin, and it shifts with leadership.

The chapter also names a cost rarely acknowledged: moral injury. Borrowed from military psychology, the term describes the distress that arises when individuals participate in actions that violate their ethical beliefs. Among sanctions professionals, moral injury does not stem from violence but from distance. Decisions made at desks ripple outward to lives unseen. When those ripples return as letters, reports, or stalled transactions, the gap between intent and effect can wound.

Several anonymised composites illustrate this burden. A licensing officer who approves fuel shipments under time pressure, knowing delay can be fatal. A compliance analyst who blocks tuition payments while following policy. A policy aide who reads field reports late at night. None of these roles fit the stereotype of moral crisis. All carry it.

Institutions rarely offer language for this experience. Performance reviews measure accuracy and timeliness. Training covers law and risk. There is little space to process guilt, ambiguity, or grief. Individuals improvise. Some compartmentalise. Some seek meaning in reform. Some leave.

This chapter does not argue that doubt invalidates sanctions. It argues that ignoring doubt weakens them. Systems that cannot hear their own architects lose precision. They become louder rather than smarter. The presence of doubters, whistleblowers, and quiet exiters is not evidence of failure alone. It is evidence of strain.

The narrative threads that follow will move between margins and meeting rooms, between those who speak and those who do not. They will show how moral unease reshapes practice long before it reshapes policy. And they will ask a question that lingers beyond this chapter: what kind of system does not merely tolerate doubt, but learns from it?

The pencil mark in the margin did not change the designation. But it changed the drafter. Over time, such marks accumulate. They form a record no archive keeps. Understanding that record is essential to understanding how sanctions endure, adapt, or fracture. The chapters ahead will not resolve this tension. They will hold it.

When insiders start to question

On 8 August 2018, in an office overlooking the Thames, a senior drafter at HM Treasury's Office of Financial Sanctions Implementation printed a consolidated designation notice and paused before signing it off. The printer hummed; the paper was warm. She took a pencil and, in the margin beside a clause on "foreseeable economic effects", wrote a small question mark. Five words only. *Who bears this cost?* The mark was light enough to be erased. It was not.

That pencil mark is the quiet beginning of doubt. It is not rebellion. It is not a leak. It is the first sign that technical mastery has outpaced moral comfort. Careers in sanctions are built on precision and speed; the paradox is that the better one becomes at the craft, the harder it can be to ignore what the craft does. Success sharpens sight.

The thesis of this section is simple and uncomfortable: cognitive dissonance accumulates most reliably inside competent systems, among people who know exactly how the machinery works. Doubt does not arrive as an external critique. It arrives as friction between outcomes and intent, measured in small, repeatable moments. The pencil becomes a motif not because it is sentimental, but because it captures how unease enters the workflow without tripping alarms.

Observe the setting. The drafter's days are governed by calendars and statutes. A designation travels from political instruction to legal text to publication, often within hours. The work rewards accuracy. It discourages reflection. Name the condition: professional compression. When timelines compress, judgement narrows. Explain the mechanism: urgency privileges legality over effect, compliance over consequence. The consequence is not malice. It is drift.

The first doubts often surface around language. Terms like "reasonably foreseeable" or "indirect benefit" are elastic by design. They allow measures to adapt to evasive behaviour. They also expand the circle of impact. In 2019, following amendments to the EU's Syria sanctions regime, humanitarian organisations reported delays at borders linked to banks' interpretations of "dual-use facilitation" (European Commission, 2019). The law had not changed dramatically; its reading had. The drafter knew this. Her pencil hovered.

Name the process: semantic load. Words carry pressure. Explain why it matters: each additional interpretive burden placed on intermediaries multiplies caution downstream. The consequence is observable behaviour. Banks slow payments. Suppliers add premiums. Aid convoys wait. None of this violates the letter of the designation. It fulfils it too well.

A second source of doubt is metrics. Sanctions programmes promise leverage, but they measure proxies. A policy analyst in Washington, working with Office of Foreign Assets Control data in 2020, attempted to correlate asset freezes with subsequent policy concessions across four regimes. The correlation was weak once confounding variables were introduced (OFAC annual report, 2020). The analyst flagged this internally. The response was polite. The programme continued. Name the phenomenon: indicator substitution. Explain it: when goals are complex, systems settle for what can be counted. The consequence is a widening gap between declared success and lived effect.

These moments do not topple belief. They erode it. The drafter's pencil marks multiplied: a question beside a definition; a bracket around a footnote citing trade data from a third country; an underline beneath "temporary". Each mark was defensible as diligence. Together, they formed a private archive of doubt.

A credible counter-example complicates the story. There are insiders who never question. Some programmes deliver clear, bounded outcomes. The 2015 Joint Comprehensive Plan of Action, whatever its later fate, produced verifiable nuclear constraints within a defined timeframe (IAEA reports, 2016). For drafters working on those measures, the alignment between intent and outcome reduced dissonance. Acknowledge the limitation: doubt is not inevitable. It is conditional. Reconcile it honestly: it arises most sharply where objectives are diffuse and duration indefinite.

Translate the abstraction into a decision. In late 2021, as secondary sanctions expanded, the drafter reviewed a clause extending liability for facilitation through correspondent banking. She knew the chain. Cabinet instruction. Legal transposition. Bank guidance. Automated filters. A blocked payment somewhere far from Whitehall. The pencil returned. The motif reappears. This time, she circled the margin note.

Name the pattern: recursive responsibility. Explain it: each layer pushes judgement down the chain while retaining authority at the top. The consequence is moral distance. Individuals experience outcomes as inevitable because they are distributed.

The accumulation of doubt changes behaviour before it changes position. Insiders begin to ask different questions in meetings. They request narrower definitions. They push for time-bound reviews. They insist on documenting humanitarian carve-outs more clearly. These are not acts of sabotage. They are attempts to reduce dissonance without breaking ranks.

Evidence of this shift appears in guidance revisions. In 2022, OFAC issued updated FAQs clarifying humanitarian transactions related to Afghanistan, explicitly addressing banks' risk perceptions (OFAC, February 2022). The change followed months of internal debate and external pressure. Insiders who had raised concerns did not leak. They persisted. Name the dynamic: incremental correction. Explain it: systems can absorb doubt as refinement when it is framed as risk reduction. The consequence is modest improvement, unevenly applied.

Yet not all doubts find expression. Some remain pencilled. The cost of speaking rises with seniority. Careers that have thrived on trust are reluctant to test it. The drafter understood this. Her annotations stayed in her drawer. Silence became a strategy.

The pencil motif returns again near the end. In 2023, reviewing a renewal clause that would extend measures indefinitely, she erased an old note and replaced it with a new one: *review effects quarterly*. Five words. It was a small victory. It was also a compromise.

The sharpened choice at the close of this section is not between loyalty and conscience. It is between treating doubt as noise or as data. Sanctions systems that dismiss internal questioning risk becoming blunt instruments. Those that read pencil marks as signals can recalibrate without collapse. The next sections follow what happens when insiders choose to speak, to stay, or to leave. The margin is not the end of the page. It is where revision begins.

Speaking out and staying silent

On 14 March 2020, a data analyst resigned from a mid-sized European bank in Frankfurt, clearing her desk while most of the building stood empty. The pandemic had already thinned the corridors; the lifts smelled faintly of disinfectant. Her exit interview lasted eleven minutes. She did not allege misconduct. She did not file a report. She thanked her manager, handed in her pass, and left behind a personal notebook that contained no proprietary data, only hand-drawn flow charts of transactions that had troubled her. One line was circled repeatedly. The circle was uneven.

This is the paradox at the heart of whistleblowing in sanctions systems: the most serious moral doubts often produce the least dramatic exits. Silence is not apathy. It is frequently a calculation.

The thesis of this section is that speaking out and staying silent are not opposites but adjacent strategies within constrained institutions. Both are shaped by assessments of risk, efficacy, and audience. Formal whistleblowing, strategic leaking, quiet resignation, and internal advocacy sit on the same continuum of response. The public scandal is the exception. The quiet departure is the norm.

Observe the analyst's role. She worked on transaction monitoring models, tuning thresholds after designation updates. In January 2020, following expanded US secondary sanctions, her team tightened filters on correspondent flows linked to a Central Asian corridor. False positives spiked. Legitimate trade payments stalled. Internal metrics showed a 38 per cent increase in blocked transactions within three weeks (internal compliance report, 2020). She flagged this. The response was procedural. Risk appetite had shifted. Name the condition: institutional asymmetry. Explain it: the cost of over-blocking is diffuse and delayed, while the cost of under-blocking is immediate and concentrated. The consequence is predictable behaviour. Systems err on the side of excess.

Her doubts sharpened around repetition. Each recalibration produced the same pattern. Each explanation cited the same enforcement fears. The analyst modelled alternative thresholds that reduced humanitarian friction without materially increasing exposure. The models were reviewed. They were shelved. Not rejected. Deferred.

Translate abstraction into choice. At this point, three paths were visible. Formal whistleblowing through internal channels. External disclosure. Exit. She assessed them sequentially.

Formal whistleblowing requires belief in corrective capacity. In regulated financial institutions, this path is structured but slow. Studies of whistleblowing in banking show that internal reports are most effective when allegations concern discrete violations, not systemic design choices (Near and Miceli, 2016). Her concern was structural. It implicated incentives, not actors. Name the barrier: category mismatch. Explain it: systems built to address breaches struggle to process critiques of architecture. The consequence is frustration without remedy.

External disclosure carries different risks. Strategic leaks can provoke rapid change, but they also narrow narratives. The analyst reviewed recent cases. The 2016 Panama Papers exposed offshore structures at scale, but their impact on sanctions enforcement was uneven, producing regulatory attention alongside defensive tightening (ICIJ, 2017). Leaks polarise. They demand villains. Her work did not offer them. It offered trade-offs.

Exit promised relief without rupture. It preserved professional reputation. It avoided legal exposure. It also limited impact. Name the calculation: constrained agency. Explain it: when the probability of change through voice is low and the cost of exposure high, exit becomes rational. The consequence is silent diffusion of expertise. Institutions lose critics without absorbing their critique.

Her decision reshaped practice indirectly. She joined a consultancy advising humanitarian organisations on banking access. Within a year, she contributed to guidance cited by several European banks when reassessing de-risking policies (EBA discussion paper, 2021). Her influence moved laterally, not vertically. The circle in her notebook closed elsewhere.

A second, named example clarifies the spectrum. In June 2014, Edward Snowden's disclosures revealed extensive surveillance programmes. Whatever one's judgement, the case illustrates the high-cost, high-impact end of whistleblowing. The disclosures forced legal and policy reforms but also exacted severe personal costs. For sanctions professionals, whose work often sits below public visibility, the calculus differs. Their disclosures would likely lack immediate resonance while attracting significant retaliation. Acknowledge the limitation: some harms justify extreme disclosure. Reconcile it: most sanctions-related doubts concern proportionality and design, not illegality.

Between exit and exposure lies quiet internal resistance. Analysts reframe memos. Lawyers add caveats. Compliance officers document exceptions meticulously. These acts rarely appear in headlines. They accumulate.

Name this pattern: subterranean reform. Explain it: change occurs through attrition of crude practices as informed staff adjust defaults. The consequence is incremental improvement without acknowledgement. It is fragile. It depends on people staying.

Why do many doubts never become scandals? Because scandal requires narrative compression. It demands clear villains and victims. Sanctions systems distribute both. The harm is real but mediated. The responsibility is shared but asymmetrical. The analyst understood this. Her story would not fit a front page.

Metrics reinforce silence. Enforcement statistics celebrate penalties avoided and fines imposed. They rarely track payments delayed or livelihoods disrupted. In 2019, global sanctions fines exceeded $1.3 billion (KPMG, 2019). The number of lawful transactions abandoned due to risk aversion was not recorded. Name the imbalance: asymmetric visibility. Explain it: what is measured commands attention. The consequence is moral opacity.

The motif of the circle returns. Circles appear in compliance dashboards as well—risk rings, exposure maps. They signal containment. The analyst's hand-drawn circle meant something else. It marked a point she could not reconcile. When she left, the circle did not vanish. It migrated.

Silence can also be strategic. Some professionals wait. They gather evidence. They build coalitions. Speaking too early forecloses influence. This is not cowardice. It is timing. A diplomat interviewed in 2022 described withholding concerns about secondary sanctions' impact on allied banks until a review window opened. When he spoke, the audience was ready. The policy adjusted marginally. Timing mattered.

Still, silence extracts a cost. Moral residue accumulates. The decision not to speak does not erase responsibility; it redistributes it inward. Over time, this produces exits. Talent drains. Institutions harden.

The sharpened choice at the close of this section is not whether whistleblowing is good or bad. It is whether systems create credible pathways for internal voice before silence becomes the least harmful option. When exit becomes the dominant response to doubt, institutions lose both critics and correctives. The next section follows those who choose to stay—and attempt reform from within—testing whether scepticism can be institutionalised without collapse.

Reformers who stay inside

On 22 September 2021, at 07:40, a compliance chief at a multinational European bank arrived early at his office in Amsterdam to review a draft internal notice before it circulated to 14,000 staff. The document concerned humanitarian transactions linked to Afghanistan. Overnight, the Taliban takeover had triggered sweeping sanctions risk alerts. Relationship managers were already asking whether to freeze everything. The draft notice did what most such notices did: it warned of exposure, cited enforcement risk, and advised extreme caution. The compliance chief changed one sentence. He replaced *avoid all transactions* with *proceed only within clearly defined humanitarian channels*. The edit reduced nothing on the balance sheet. It altered behaviour.

This is the counter-paradox to whistleblowing: scepticism can be a source of institutional strength when it is exercised from within. The question is not whether insiders doubt, but whether systems allow doubt to become design.

The thesis of this section is that reformers who stay inside sanctions architectures operate through credibility rather than confrontation. They translate ethical unease into procedural change. Their scepticism does not corrode authority; it refines it. The cost is patience. The risk is co-option. The reward, when it comes, is durability.

Observe the compliance chief's position. He had spent twenty-five years in banking, including a decade building sanctions frameworks across multiple jurisdictions. Regulators knew his name. Auditors trusted his judgement. He had survived enforcement scares by being conservative. That history mattered. Name the asset: accumulated credibility. Explain it: institutions listen to critics who have previously protected them. The consequence is leverage without spectacle.

His doubts were not sudden. They matured across crises. In 2018, after the reimposition of US sanctions on Iran, his bank terminated correspondent relationships with several regional institutions to reduce exposure. The decision complied with guidance. It also cut off remittance corridors used by diaspora families. Complaints reached his desk. He reviewed them personally. The pattern repeated: lawful payments, blocked pre-emptively. Name the phenomenon: anticipatory closure. Explain it: fear of secondary sanctions encourages institutions to withdraw before rules require it. The consequence is de facto sanctions beyond policy intent.

Instead of objecting publicly, he mapped the decision chain. Where did fear enter? At which approval stage did caution turn absolute? He discovered that front-line teams lacked clear examples of permitted transactions. Guidance existed, but it was abstract. The solution was mundane. He commissioned case-based training built around real humanitarian scenarios, vetted by regulators informally before rollout. Within six months, blocked humanitarian payments fell by 27 per cent without an increase in alerts escalated to regulators (internal compliance metrics, 2019). Skepticism became calibration.

Name this strategy: internal translation. Explain it: reformers rephrase policy intent into operational language that reduces defensive interpretation. The consequence is narrower application without public conflict.

A second, checkable example reinforces the point. In 2022, following criticism of over-compliance affecting aid flows to Syria, the US Treasury issued expanded General License 23, clarifying permissible humanitarian activities (US Treasury, February 2023). The licence did not emerge fully formed. It followed sustained engagement by compliance leaders, NGOs, and policy staff who framed the problem as operational friction rather than moral failure. Reform came through persistence, not protest.

The compliance chief played this game deliberately. He avoided moralising language. He spoke in the grammar of risk. He argued that indiscriminate blocking increased reputational exposure and regulatory scrutiny. He produced metrics. He aligned scepticism with institutional interest.

Translate abstraction into behaviour. When new designations arrived, he convened cross-functional reviews that included legal, compliance, and front-line teams. He insisted on writing guidance that fit on one page. He required examples. He challenged unnecessary breadth. Each act was small. Together, they shifted defaults.

The motif here is the filter. Sanctions systems rely on filters—legal, technical, cognitive. Reformers adjust their mesh. Too coarse, and harm spreads. Too fine, and enforcement fails. The compliance chief understood that filters are not neutral. They embody judgement.

A credible limitation complicates the narrative. Staying inside carries risks. Reformers can become buffers, absorbing criticism without effecting change. Institutions may showcase them as evidence of responsibility while maintaining harmful practices elsewhere. Acknowledge this honestly. In some regimes, particularly those driven by geopolitics rather than regulation, internal reform has limited reach. The compliance chief failed repeatedly to influence decisions tied to high-profile enforcement actions. Reconcile it: internal reform is contingent. It works best where regulators tolerate nuance.

Another named example illustrates this boundary. In the early 2000s, UN sanctions on Iraq included humanitarian exemptions under the Oil-for-Food Programme. Internal critics raised concerns about both humanitarian impact and corruption. Some reforms were implemented. Others were ignored until scandal forced overhaul (UN Independent Inquiry Committee, 2005). The lesson is sobering. Staying inside can delay reckoning as well as improve practice.

Why, then, do some reformers persist? Because exit forfeits influence, and whistleblowing collapses complexity into accusation. For those with long institutional memory, staying is a bet that systems can learn.

The compliance chief's most consequential intervention came quietly. In late 2021, he persuaded his bank to pilot a *humanitarian fast-track* for licensing queries, committing to responses within seventy-two hours. The process reduced delays for urgent medical payments. It also generated data. That data fed back into policy discussions with regulators. The filter tightened where it should and loosened where it could.

Name the effect: reflexive governance. Explain it: systems improve when feedback loops include those affected by rules. The consequence is adaptability without abandonment.

The filter motif returns at the close. Reformers do not remove filters. They retune them. Their work is rarely celebrated. It is often misunderstood by critics who demand rupture. Yet its impact endures because it is embedded.

The sharpened choice at the end of this section is whether institutions treat scepticism as threat or resource. When doubt is punished, it leaks or leaves. When it is harnessed, it becomes design. The final section of this chapter turns to those for whom staying is no longer possible, and to the quieter injuries that persist even when reform succeeds.

Living with moral injury

On 12 November 2019, the American Psychiatric Association hosted a closed-door workshop in Washington, DC, on moral injury, a concept first articulated by Jonathan Shay in the 1990s to describe psychic harm among combat veterans. The room smelled faintly of coffee and carpet cleaner. Among the clinicians sat two people who were not clinicians at all: a former sanctions analyst from the US Treasury and a compliance manager from a European bank. Neither spoke publicly. Both took notes. The invitation itself was an admission that harm can travel without violence.

Moral injury names a paradox: people can be injured by actions they did not intend, carried out at a distance, under authority they respected. It is not trauma. It is accounting. A quiet reckoning. Five-word sentence, early and exact: *The numbers never stayed put.*

The thesis of this section is that sanctions professionals experience moral injury precisely because their work succeeds technically. The better the system functions, the more distant the harm appears, and the harder it becomes to integrate responsibility. Institutions rarely recognise this burden because it does not register as misconduct or failure. Individuals are left to balance the ledger alone.

Observe the first composite. Call her A. She worked in a national sanctions authority, drafting designation packages. Her days were structured and calm. Meetings. Citations. Deadlines. In 2017, after a tranche of designations linked to a regional conflict, she began receiving aggregated humanitarian impact reports from an external agency. The reports were anonymised. They showed medicine shortages correlated with banking restrictions. The correlation was not causation. She knew this. She also knew that correlation was all the system allowed her to see.

Name the condition: remote culpability. Explain it: when harm is mediated through layers of legality and automation, responsibility feels both diluted and inescapable. The consequence is cognitive strain. A found herself replaying drafting decisions at night, not because they were wrong, but because they were consequential.

Translate abstraction into behaviour. She began re-reading footnotes. She delayed sign-off by hours to request clarifications that rarely changed outcomes. She stopped volunteering for fast-track assignments. None of this breached protocol. It slowed her.

A second composite, B, worked in a global bank's sanctions screening team in London. His metrics were clear: alerts resolved per hour, false positives reduced, audits passed. In 2020, after sanctions expanded rapidly, his team cleared record volumes. Complaints rose in parallel. Customers wrote about tuition payments stuck, salaries unpaid. He read the emails. He could not reply. The policy forbade it.

Name the experience: enforced muteness. Explain it: systems that centralise authority often silence those closest to effects. The consequence is moral residue—unexpressed concern that accumulates.

B developed rituals. He jogged at night. He avoided news. He told himself that regulators set the rules. The ledger motif enters here. He imagined a ledger in which debits and credits never reconciled. He did not know where to post the entries.

The term moral injury helps because it distinguishes guilt from wrongdoing. Shay defined it as a betrayal of "what's right" by legitimate authority in high-stakes situations (Shay, 1994). Sanctions professionals fit the frame imperfectly but instructively. The betrayal is subtle. Authority does not command harm; it normalises trade-offs. The stakes are high; the battlefield is abstract.

Evidence supports the extension. Studies of moral injury among non-military professionals—healthcare workers, humanitarian staff—show similar patterns of distress linked to systemic constraints rather than personal error (Litz et al., 2009). Sanctions work shares the structure: duty-bound action, limited agency, significant downstream impact.

A credible counter-example tempers the argument. Some professionals do not experience moral injury. They compartmentalise successfully. They view sanctions as necessary tools and accept collateral effects as unavoidable. This is not denial; it is worldview. Reconcile it: moral injury depends on values alignment. Those whose moral frameworks prioritise deterrence over distributive justice report less strain. The injury is not universal.

A third composite, C, complicates matters further. C was a senior policy adviser involved in sanctions design. He travelled occasionally to sanctioned countries as part of diplomatic delegations. In 2018, in a hospital corridor in a Middle Eastern capital, he spoke with doctors who described equipment shortages linked to banking restrictions. The visit lasted one afternoon. The memory lasted years.

Name the trigger: embodied encounter. Explain it: first-hand testimony collapses abstraction. The consequence is recalibration of self-concept. C returned and pushed for narrower designations. Some succeeded. Others did not. The ledger gained entries on both sides.

Institutions respond poorly to moral injury because it resists categorisation. It is not burnout, though exhaustion may follow. It is not dissent, though it may lead there. Human resources frameworks offer resilience training. Ethics committees review compliance. Neither addresses injury caused by lawful action with harmful effects.

Metrics again obscure. Institutions track enforcement success and compliance failures. They do not track moral cost. In 2021, an internal survey at a large financial institution reported elevated stress among compliance staff, but the findings were aggregated under "workload pressure" (industry survey, 2021). The language flattened meaning.

Translate this into consequence. When moral injury goes unnamed, individuals personalise it. They assume weakness. They exit quietly. Talent drains. Institutional memory thins. Systems become more brittle.

The ledger motif returns a second time. A kept a private spreadsheet listing designations she had worked on and subsequent humanitarian reports. She never shared it. It was not evidence. It was an attempt to balance accounts that the institution did not keep.

A limitation deserves acknowledgement. Overemphasising moral injury risks moral inflation. Sanctions are tools of statecraft. Harm is not equivalent to violence. Professionals are not victims in the same sense as those affected on the ground. Reconcile this carefully. Moral injury does not claim equivalence. It claims consequence. It explains why lawful power can wound those who wield it.

Some coping strategies mitigate injury. Peer discussion helps when permitted. Rotations reduce exposure. Clearer humanitarian guidance eases strain by aligning intent and effect. These are partial. They depend on institutional will.

Others choose exit. They move to academia, NGOs, consultancy. The injury does not vanish. It transforms. Distance brings relief. It also brings lingering questions. Did staying longer help? Did leaving absolve anything? The ledger remains open.

The motif appears a final time near the close. Moral injury is unresolved accounting. Systems that refuse to keep the books force individuals to do it alone.

The sharpened choice at the end of this chapter is diagnostic rather than prescriptive. If sanctions architectures are to endure without hollowing out their builders, they must recognise moral cost as a design variable, not a personal failing. The next chapter turns outward again, to imagine pressure that is effective without blindness, and architects who can work without carrying ledgers no one else will read.

Chapter 10 Reimagining Pressure Without Blindness

In late May 2016, in a conference room overlooking Lake Geneva, a small group of officials argued over a spreadsheet that refused to behave. The figures tracked fuel imports, hospital generator uptime, and electricity outages across a sanctioned economy. The data came from different sources and did not line up cleanly. A diplomat tapped the table. A development economist frowned. A sanctions lawyer, sleeves rolled, asked whether the problem was the numbers or the assumptions beneath them. Outside, the lake was calm. Inside, something was shifting: pressure was being reconsidered as a design problem rather than a reflex.

The paradox that opens this chapter is not whether sanctions work, but why they so often become the only answer once invoked. Pressure, once applied, tends to crowd out alternatives. It simplifies choice. It also dulls sight. The architects gathered in Geneva were not rejecting coercion; they were questioning its default settings. The spreadsheet, stubborn and incomplete, forced the issue.

This chapter advances a forward-looking claim rooted in everything that has come before: systems built to exert pressure can be redesigned to see more clearly without surrendering force. Blindness is not intrinsic to sanctions. It is an artefact of habit, incentive, and institutional memory. When those elements shift, so does the tool.

Across earlier chapters, the reader has met the builders of chokepoints, the hunters of evasion, the gatekeepers of compliance, and the doubters who stayed or left. Their stories converge here. Not in a manifesto, but in a series of experiments, some tentative, some quietly radical, that suggest how pressure might be applied with discrimination rather than bluntness. The move is not from coercion to compassion, but from automaticity to choice.

The first step in reimagining pressure is recognising that sanctions are not the only instrument available to states seeking leverage. They are, however, the most modular. They can be scaled, targeted, automated, and exported. This versatility explains their appeal. It also explains their overuse. When a tool fits many hands, it tends to be picked up often.

Yet even within institutions most associated with financial coercion, alternatives have long circulated. Diplomatic bargains that trade phased relief for verifiable steps. Positive incentives that reward compliance rather than punish defiance. Narrowly targeted measures that focus on specific behaviours instead of entire economies. These options are not new. What is new is the willingness of some architects to combine them deliberately, resisting the gravitational pull of ever-expanding lists and tightening filters.

Consider a sanctions adviser seconded to a foreign ministry in 2018, tasked with responding to repeated violations by a mid-level state actor. The usual playbook pointed towards escalation: more designations, broader financial restrictions. Instead, the adviser proposed a mixed strategy. Limited new sanctions were paired with explicit offers of relief tied to concrete actions, communicated privately through intermediaries rather than publicly through press releases. The approach unsettled colleagues. It also produced movement where previous rounds had stalled. The lesson was not that incentives replace pressure, but that sequencing matters.

Name the shift: compositional design. Explain it: pressure works differently when combined with credible exits. The consequence is optionality. Targets can respond without humiliation. Enforcers can recalibrate without losing face.

Such experiments rarely announce themselves. They circulate as anecdotes, memos, and draft talking points shared among practitioners who have learned, often painfully, what overreach costs. Out of this circulation has emerged a loose, informal body of design principles for what some now call humane sanctions. The term is contested. It risks sentimentality. Practitioners tend to prefer plainer language: precision, proportionality, reversibility.

These principles did not descend from law reviews. They rose from practice. A compliance chief shares a template for humanitarian fast-tracks. A policy aide insists on sunset clauses tied to reviewable indicators. A risk officer argues that narrower designations reduce over-compliance and therefore improve effectiveness. None of this reads as reformist rhetoric. It reads as operational wisdom.

Name the dynamic: bottom-up norming. Explain it: when formal reform stalls, informal standards fill the gap. The consequence is uneven change, but real change nonetheless. Institutions begin to expect clearer rationales, better data, and more explicit trade-offs.

One illustrative network emerged quietly after 2020, linking sanctions practitioners across governments, banks, and humanitarian organisations. They met under Chatham House rules, swapped redacted case studies, and debated failure modes. There were no communiqués. There was, however, convergence around a few ideas: designations should be narrower than politically comfortable; humanitarian exceptions should be written for banks, not just lawyers; feedback should arrive while it still matters. These ideas travelled faster than formal guidance ever could.

Reimagining pressure also requires expanding who gets to speak. Throughout this book, the voices of those affected by sanctions have appeared indirectly, mediated through reports, complaints, and rare visits. The imbalance has been structural. Policy debates privilege expertise over experience. This chapter examines attempts to rebalance that equation without collapsing into performative listening.

One such attempt involved consultative panels composed of diaspora representatives, humanitarian operators, and trade specialists, convened to review the effects of specific measures. The panels had no veto. They had access. Their testimony did not override security concerns. It complicated them. In one case, feedback from a panel led to a technical amendment that unblocked tuition payments without altering the core sanction. The change did not make headlines. It changed lives.

Name the mechanism: structured listening. Explain it: systems see differently when experience is treated as data. The consequence is friction in the best sense—resistance that improves fit.

Sceptics worry, reasonably, about capture and delay. Opening deliberation risks politicisation. It can slow response. These concerns are real. They are not fatal. The experiments that endured were those that bounded participation clearly and tied it to specific review points. Listening was not endless. It was scheduled.

As pressure becomes more discriminating, the role of the architect changes. The final movement of this chapter asks what kind of professional identity is required to sustain these shifts. The composite figure that emerges from earlier profiles is not a saint or a technocrat alone. It is someone fluent in law and data, comfortable with ambiguity, and capable of ethical imagination without paralysis.

Ethical imagination here does not mean moralising. It means the capacity to picture downstream effects and to treat them as design inputs rather than regrettable externalities. It means asking, before a filter is tightened or a designation broadened, who will bear the cost and whether that cost advances the stated aim. These questions do not weaken pressure. They discipline it.

There is a risk in this vision. Architects who see too much may hesitate too long. The world does not pause for perfect design. This chapter does not propose hesitation as virtue. It proposes awareness as competence.

The Geneva spreadsheet returns near the close. The group did not resolve every inconsistency. They agreed on fewer certainties than they had hoped. They also agreed on something more durable: pressure should be adjustable, not cumulative by default. Blindness was a choice. So was sight.

The momentum leaving this chapter is deliberately forward-facing. The systems described in earlier pages are not immutable. They are built, maintained, and revised by people whose choices, taken together, shape outcomes far beyond their desks. Reimagining pressure without blindness is not an abstract aspiration. It is a set of practices already underway, uneven and incomplete, but real. The question is not whether they will replace sanctions. It is whether they will redefine how sanctions are conceived, applied, and lived with—by those who enforce them and those who endure them.

Alternative tools and mixed strategies

On 14 July 2015, in Vienna, the Joint Comprehensive Plan of Action was announced after twenty months of negotiation between Iran and the P5+1. One figure framed the bargain with brutal clarity: roughly US$100 billion in frozen Iranian assets would be unfrozen in stages, contingent on verified nuclear constraints, monitored by the International Atomic Energy Agency. The sum was not a gift. It was leverage returned under conditions. For sanctions architects watching from Washington, Brussels, and Tehran, the episode posed a disquieting question. If pressure could be partially lifted to secure compliance, why had it so often been treated as an all-or-nothing instrument?

Pressure is not a switch.
It is a dimmer.

That dimmer—this chapter's guiding image—captures a reality long obscured by rhetoric. Financial sanctions, trade controls, and blacklists are adjustable technologies. Yet institutional habit encourages binary thinking: impose or lift, tighten or waive. The thesis advanced here is straightforward and unfashionable. Mixed strategies, combining coercion with inducement and narrow targeting, often outperform broad financial pressure alone, not because they are softer, but because they are legible to those meant to respond.

Observe the pattern that recurs across sanctions regimes. Broad measures are imposed to signal resolve. Compliance proves elusive. Pressure escalates. Humanitarian costs mount. Eventually, negotiators search for exits, assembling ad hoc relief packages that sit uneasily alongside the original design. Name the problem: coercive saturation. Explain it: once pressure becomes totalising, it ceases to communicate priorities. The consequence is stalemate.

Architects who have resisted this pattern have tended to do so quietly, working inside the system rather than against it. Their experiments rarely displace sanctions. They recompose them. Diplomatic bargains, positive incentives, and narrowly targeted measures are not alternatives to pressure so much as instruments that modulate it. The dimmer matters.

Diplomatic bargains are the most visible of these tools, and the most politically fraught. They require governments to admit that pressure is a means rather than an end. The JCPOA remains the clearest modern example. Its design logic was explicit. Sanctions relief would be reversible. Verification would be intrusive. Incentives would be staged. The bargain's fragility—exposed by the United States' withdrawal in May 2018—does not negate the design insight. It sharpens it. When relief lacks durability, incentives lose credibility. That is a failure of commitment, not of mixed strategy.

A less discussed case unfolded in Sudan. In January 2017, the US Treasury announced the revocation of comprehensive sanctions imposed two decades earlier, citing improvements in humanitarian access and counterterrorism cooperation. The measures were replaced with targeted designations and ongoing monitoring. The decision followed a six-month general licence that functioned as a test. Exports increased. Banks cautiously re-engaged. The signal was conditional normalisation. Here, inducement preceded full relief. The consequence was not transformation, but movement.

Positive incentives need not take the form of asset releases or market access. They can be procedural. A licensing fast-track for compliant actors. Public recognition for verified behaviour changes. Quiet assurances to banks that specific corridors are safe. These measures rarely attract attention, which is partly their strength. They alter cost-benefit calculations without inviting domestic backlash.

Consider a case officer within a European foreign ministry in 2019, tasked with responding to repeated breaches by a state-owned shipping firm. Rather than proposing additional designations, she worked with port authorities to offer expedited clearance for vessels that adopted new transparency standards. The incentive was operational, not financial. Compliance improved. The firm's competitors followed. Name the tactic: behavioural targeting. Explain it: incentives tied to observable actions travel faster than abstract threats. The consequence is diffusion.

Narrow targeting is the third pillar of mixed strategies, and the most technically demanding. It requires sanctions designers to identify which nodes matter and which do not. Broad financial pressure relies on scale. Narrow measures rely on precision. The distinction is not moral. It is functional.

The United States' use of sectoral sanctions on Russia after 2014 illustrates the point. Rather than blocking all transactions, the measures restricted access to long-term financing for specific energy and defence firms. The design preserved short-term trade while constraining investment horizons. According to analysis by the Peterson Institute for International Economics (Guriev and Itskhoki, 2015), the impact on Russia's GDP was significant but less disruptive to European supply chains than comprehensive trade bans would have been. The dimmer was set deliberately.

Critics argue that narrow targeting invites evasion. Sometimes it does. That is the credible limitation of mixed strategies. Precision can be gamed. Actors adapt. Shell companies proliferate. Reconciling this limitation requires two moves. First, accept that no design eliminates evasion entirely. Second, pair targeting with monitoring. Precision without feedback is naïveté. Precision with feedback is governance.

Feedback mechanisms have been discussed elsewhere in this book. Their relevance here is direct. Mixed strategies depend on information flows. Diplomatic bargains require verification. Incentives require measurement. Narrow measures require updating. Without these, the dimmer sticks.

The tendency to default to sanctions persists not because alternatives are unknown, but because they are institutionally awkward. Sanctions fit existing workflows. They are legible to legislatures. They externalise risk. Mixed strategies do the opposite. They demand coordination across departments, sustained attention, and tolerance for ambiguity. These are scarce resources.

Yet even within sanctions-heavy institutions, some actors have sought to conserve them. An architect seconded to a multilateral development bank described the challenge plainly. "Pressure is easy to sell," he said. "Design is harder." His team experimented with what they called *conditional access*: allowing limited participation in development programmes for entities that met governance benchmarks, even while broader sanctions remained. The results were uneven. They were also instructive. Where access was credible, behaviour shifted. Where it was not, nothing changed.

Name the insight: credibility trumps severity. Explain it: actors respond to signals they believe will endure. The consequence is strategic patience.

This patience runs counter to crisis politics. When violations occur, the demand is for visible response. Sanctions satisfy that demand. Mixed strategies often do not. Their effects are incremental. Their successes are contestable. Their failures are easy to politicise. This asymmetry explains why architects who favour them tend to operate below the radar.

The motif returns. The dimmer works best in rooms where someone stays to adjust it.

The choice between broad pressure and mixed strategies is not absolute. It is temporal. Broad measures may be necessary to arrest behaviour. Mixed strategies may be necessary to change it. The sequence matters. So does the exit. Pressure without an off-ramp invites defiance. Incentives without pressure invite delay. The art lies in combination.

A final example brings the argument home. In 2020, amid global disruptions, a coalition of states faced repeated sanctions breaches by a regional power. Initial responses followed the script: additional listings, louder warnings. Progress stalled. A small group of advisers proposed a recalibration. Targeted relief on non-core exports, tied to verifiable steps, accompanied by a pause in new designations. The proposal met resistance. It also worked. Not completely. Enough.

The sharpened choice at the close of this subchapter is this. Architects can continue to treat sanctions as the default language of pressure, adjusting only volume. Or they can learn to speak in sentences, combining coercion, inducement, and precision to convey meaning. The testable next step is modest: before recommending new broad measures, require designers to articulate what incentive, however small, accompanies them, and how it will be delivered. If the dimmer is never used, it will seize.

Design principles for humane sanctions

On 17 December 2019, in Geneva, a draft guidance note circulated quietly among officials from three governments and two multilateral agencies. It carried no crest and no classification, only a footer with a number: 72. That was the count of humanitarian payment delays reported in one quarter by a single international charity, each delay traced not to illegality but to risk aversion by intermediaries. The document's author, a legal adviser seconded to the United Nations Office for the Coordination of Humanitarian Affairs, did not propose new law. She proposed restraint.

Seventy-two blocked transfers.
No law was broken.

The paradox sits at the heart of humane sanctions design. Harm often arises not from what rules say, but from how systems respond to them. The central thesis of this subchapter is that humane sanctions are not primarily a matter of ethical intent or political rhetoric. They are a matter of design discipline, informed by practice, refined by feedback, and shared horizontally long before it is codified vertically.

Across the biographies traced in this book, a pattern emerges. Practitioners who succeed in reducing civilian harm rarely do so by overturning sanctions regimes. They do so by embedding small design principles—informal, sometimes invisible—that act as *circuit breakers* within systems prone to runaway caution. This motif, the circuit breaker, binds the argument that follows. Humane sanctions are those designed to trip before damage propagates.

Observe the informal network that has taken shape over the past decade. It has no charter and no secretariat. Its members are mid-career officials: licensing officers, compliance leads, humanitarian lawyers, and policy advisers who have rotated between capitals and institutions. They meet at the margins of conferences, exchange drafts by encrypted email, and trade war stories over coffee. Name the phenomenon: distributed design. Explain it: when formal reform stalls, practice evolves laterally. The consequence is a shadow curriculum of restraint.

One principle recurs in their exchanges. Precision beats breadth. This is not a moral slogan. It is an operational insight. Broad measures increase uncertainty. Uncertainty triggers defensive behaviour. Defensive behaviour amplifies harm. The circuit breaker here is scope discipline. Sanctions that specify who is targeted, why, and under what conditions relief applies reduce the interpretive burden on intermediaries.

A concrete example comes from the European Union's 2020 amendments to its Syria regime. Following extensive consultations with humanitarian organisations, the EU clarified that certain categories of medical equipment fell outside existing controls. The change did not alter the headline sanctions. It altered definitions. According to Médecins Sans Frontières (2021), procurement delays for those items fell measurably in the following year. Name the mechanism: definitional hygiene. Explain it: clarity narrows discretion. The consequence is throughput.

A second principle concerns temporal design. Humane sanctions recognise time as a variable, not a backdrop. Delays kill as surely as prohibitions. Practitioners therefore advocate for built-in review points and automatic renewals for humanitarian licences. The absence of such features shifts risk onto the most vulnerable actors.

In 2018, the US Treasury's Office of Foreign Assets Control introduced a general licence authorising certain activities in Venezuela related to telecommunications and internet services. Crucially, the licence carried an automatic renewal clause, subject to revocation. This design choice signalled continuity. Banks responded accordingly. The circuit breaker here was predictability. When rules persist by default, fear recedes.

A credible limitation must be acknowledged. Automaticity can entrench outdated permissions. Reconciling this requires pairing renewal with data. Licences that renew should also report. Feedback transforms inertia into oversight.

A third principle emerges from the biographies: proximity to impact. Humane design insists that those crafting measures remain close to their effects. Distance breeds abstraction. Abstraction breeds indifference. Practitioners counter this by institutionalising listening.

One member of the informal network described a practice she called *reverse briefings*. Before finalising a sanctions package, her team would invite humanitarian field staff to explain how similar measures had played out on the ground. These sessions carried no veto power. They carried weight. The consequence was not paralysis but adjustment: narrower carve-outs, clearer guidance, fewer surprises. The circuit breaker here was narrative intrusion. Stories interrupt models.

Evidence supports the value of this intrusion. A study by the International Committee of the Red Cross (2019) found that sanctions regimes incorporating formal consultation mechanisms were associated with fewer reported access impediments, controlling for context. The finding does not prove causation. It suggests correlation worth designing for.

A fourth principle concerns accountability inside institutions. Humane sanctions are not self-executing. They depend on individuals who can raise concerns without career suicide. Practitioners therefore stress the importance of protected dissent.

In 2021, a multilateral development bank introduced an internal review panel empowered to flag potential humanitarian risks associated with sanctions-related decisions. The panel's recommendations were non-binding. Their existence altered behaviour. Files improved. Assumptions were documented. The circuit breaker was procedural friction, inserted deliberately to slow decisions that might otherwise rush harm.

Translate the abstraction. Friction is often framed as inefficiency. Here, it is care.

The fifth principle is humility about knowledge. Sanctions designers operate in complex systems. Outcomes are overdetermined. Humane design resists claims of certainty. It favours reversibility.

This principle was evident in the United Kingdom's approach to its post-Brexit sanctions framework. The Sanctions and Anti-Money Laundering Act 2018 included provisions for periodic review and sunset clauses. These features did not weaken the regime. They acknowledged fallibility. The circuit breaker was the off-switch.

Critics argue that such humility signals weakness. This objection misunderstands power. The ability to revise is strength. Rigidity courts error.

Two named examples illustrate how practice-based wisdom precedes formal reform. The first comes from the Financial Action Task Force. Long criticised for contributing to de-risking, the FATF began, in 2017, to emphasise proportionality and financial inclusion in its guidance. This shift followed years of informal advocacy by practitioners who had documented the unintended consequences of blunt compliance. Formal language followed practice.

The second comes from the World Bank's work on correspondent banking. After internal teams compiled evidence of account closures in small economies, the Bank convened a task force that issued recommendations in 2018 aimed at preserving access while managing risk. Again, the sequence mattered. Field reports preceded policy.

The credible limitation returns. Informal networks lack democratic legitimacy. Their influence can be uneven. Reconciling this requires transparency. Humane design principles must migrate from margins to mandates. Practice can lead, but law must catch up.

The motif of the circuit breaker returns for the final time. Electrical systems assume failure. They are built to fail safely. Sanctions regimes should do the same. When pressure overloads, something should trip before civilians bear the cost.

The sharpened choice facing architects is therefore not whether sanctions can be humane in theory. It is whether they will be designed as systems that anticipate harm and interrupt it. The testable next step is concrete. Before any new regime is adopted, require designers to specify which circuit breakers are in place: where clarity limits discretion, where time limits force review, where voices from the field intrude, where dissent is protected, and where reversal is possible. If none can be named, the design is incomplete.

Giving voice to those affected

On 14 March 2021, in Amman, a pilot consultative panel convened under the auspices of the Norwegian Refugee Council brought together aid workers, traders, teachers, and small-business owners living under an active sanctions regime. The budget for the exercise was modest—€180,000—but the outcome unsettled assumptions held in distant capitals. Participants did not argue against pressure in the abstract. They described how it landed. The datum that lingered in the briefing note was simple: remittances took, on average, forty-seven days longer to arrive after a regulatory update that had never mentioned civilians. Forty-seven days.

Voices travelled farther than data.

The thesis of this section is that sanctions design changes when affected communities are treated as sources of evidence rather than objects of concern. Bringing voices into the room does not dilute pressure; it re-aims it. The difference lies not in empathy as sentiment, but in testimony as method. When experience counts, design adjusts.

Observe the prevailing architecture. Sanctions debates traditionally privilege actors who speak the language of states: diplomats, lawyers, economists. Those who bear indirect costs appear, if at all, as statistics. Name the gap: representational asymmetry. Explain it: systems weight inputs by proximity to power, not proximity to impact. The consequence is predictable. Measures optimise for compliance clarity while obscuring lived effects.

The Amman panel disrupted this pattern by design. Its organisers imposed structure: timed interventions, thematic prompts, anonymised aggregation. This was not an open microphone. It was a listening exercise with rules. Participants described blocked school fees, frozen payrolls, delayed spare parts. They also described adaptation. One trader explained how goods rerouted through a neighbouring state raised prices by twelve per cent. That figure appeared nowhere in official models. The circuit breaker motif from the previous section finds a sibling here: the *listening valve*. When pressure builds, testimony releases information.

A second named example underscores the point. In June 2019, the United Nations Security Council's Panel of Experts on the Democratic People's Republic of Korea held structured interviews in Beijing and Vladivostok with humanitarian agencies operating near the border. The place mattered. So did the date. Those interviews informed subsequent guidance clarifying permissible aid activities. According to the UN Office for the Coordination of Humanitarian Affairs (2020), approvals accelerated thereafter. Name the mechanism: proximity hearing. Explain it: when designers hear effects early, they adjust thresholds. The consequence was operational relief without policy retreat.

A credible limitation deserves attention. Voices are partial. They can be strategic. Communities adapt narratives to secure relief. Reconciling this requires triangulation. Testimony must sit alongside trade data, banking reports, and field verification. Listening is necessary, not sufficient.

Translate the abstraction into practice. Effective mechanisms share three features. First, they are structured. Unbounded consultations privilege the loudest. Second, they are insulated. Participants must speak without fear of reprisal. Third, they are iterative. One-off hearings become theatre. Repetition builds signal.

An experiment by the Swiss State Secretariat for Economic Affairs illustrates these features. Beginning in 2020, SECO convened quarterly virtual sessions with Swiss NGOs and diaspora representatives affected by sanctions in the Middle East. Inputs were anonymised and coded. Over four sessions, recurring issues emerged around insurance and shipping. SECO responded with clarifications circulated to banks. According to SECO's 2022 report, transaction rejections fell in the following quarters. Name the principle: feedback integration. Explain it: repeated listening converts anecdotes into patterns. The consequence is targeted adjustment.

The motif returns. The listening valve must be calibrated. Too open, and noise overwhelms. Too closed, and pressure distorts.

A third example broadens the frame beyond humanitarian contexts. In 2018, the World Bank's Global Findex team incorporated questions on access to financial services in sanctioned environments, drawing on surveys conducted in Lebanon and Jordan. While not a consultative panel, the exercise elevated affected users as data points. The findings challenged assumptions about substitution channels. Policymakers cited the results in internal reviews. Experience entered the ledger.

Why does this matter now? Because sanctions increasingly operate through complex networks where indirect effects dominate. Designers cannot observe these effects from balance sheets alone. They require sensors. Voices are sensors.

Name the philosophical shift. It is epistemic humility. Explain it: acknowledging that those who live with rules know something essential about them. The consequence is not paralysis but precision.

Resistance persists. Some officials fear that consultation invites capture or slows response. These concerns merit respect. Yet the evidence suggests the opposite. Structured listening accelerates learning. It reduces the need for blunt revisions later. It sharpens pressure earlier.

Consider the paradox at the heart of sanctions. They aim to influence elites by constraining systems that sustain them. Those systems also sustain civilians. Without testimony, designers infer effects indirectly. Inference lags. Voices compress the lag.

A subtle but crucial benefit emerges. When communities are heard, legitimacy improves. Compliance follows legitimacy. Banks and firms, uncertain about intent, take cues from process. Transparent listening signals seriousness about mitigation. Fear recedes. Over-compliance eases.

The credible limitation returns once more. Not all voices can be included. Language, access, and security constrain participation. Reconciling this requires proxies. Trusted intermediaries, rotating panels, and mixed methods can extend reach without false claims of representativeness.

The listening valve motif echoes again. Valves require maintenance. They clog. Designers must revisit who speaks and who is missing. Otherwise, old biases reassert themselves.

The sharpened choice for future architects is clear. Treat affected communities as variables to be estimated, or as witnesses to be heard. The testable next step is modest and concrete. For every new sanctions package, require a documented plan for structured listening: who will be heard, how often, with what protections, and how inputs will alter design. If the plan cannot be written, the architecture remains blind.

What kind of architect we need next

On 3 May 2022, in Brussels, the European Commission circulated an internal review noting that more than €1.1 billion in humanitarian exemptions approved since 2018 had not translated into equivalent aid flows on the ground. The number was precise. The conclusion was not. Officials could not say whether the shortfall reflected bank behaviour, licensing delays, trade disruption, or all three. The document named no villain. It revealed a gap in authorship. Someone had designed the rules. No one had designed the learning.

Precision without imagination fails.

The thesis here is simple and demanding: the next generation of sanctions architects must combine technical mastery with ethical imagination, or the tool will continue to oscillate between bluntness and blindness. This is not a call for softer pressure. It is a call for better authorship. Systems do not drift accidentally. They drift because individual choices compound.

Observe the professional profile that dominates sanctions work today. It prizes legal exactness, procedural defensibility, and risk aversion. These traits are rational. They protect institutions. Name the pattern: compliance-first authorship. Explain it: careers advance by avoiding error, not by reducing harm. The consequence is a system optimised for survivability rather than outcomes.

Across the earlier chapters, a counter-profile emerged in fragments. The data specialist who questioned thresholds. The compliance chief who narrowed designations. The investigator who listened twice. None rejected pressure. All rejected indifference. Taken together, they sketch a composite figure. Call it the *reflective architect.*

The reflective architect begins with craft. She understands balance sheets, shipping manifests, ownership graphs, and legal texts. She can draft an exclusion protocol that survives judicial review. She can speak to banks in their own idiom. This is table stakes. Without it, imagination floats unmoored. Consequence follows: credibility grants access.

But craft alone reproduces the present. The distinguishing feature is orientation. The reflective architect treats sanctions not as events but as systems with feedback. Earlier we named the circuit breaker. Here the motif shifts slightly. Think of a *compass.* Not a map. A compass does not tell you where you are. It tells you whether you are still heading where you meant to go.

One named example clarifies the point. In 2016, Adam Szubin, then Acting Under Secretary for Terrorism and Financial Intelligence at the US Treasury, publicly warned that sanctions overreach could undermine their own effectiveness, urging precision to preserve legitimacy (US Treasury, 2016). The remark was notable not for its novelty but for its source. A technocrat spoke of restraint. Observe the behaviour: signalling limits from within power. Name it: anticipatory moderation. Explain it: leaders shape norms by articulating trade-offs before crisis. The consequence was internal space for narrower tools.

A second example comes from a different institutional culture. In 2020, the UK's Office of Financial Sanctions Implementation quietly expanded its guidance on humanitarian payments following consultations with banks and NGOs. The change attracted little press. According to OFSI's Annual Review (2021), enquiries declined while licence processing times improved. The architect here was not a single author but a team that valued iteration. Name the quality: institutional patience. Explain it: willingness to revise without spectacle. The consequence was functional relief without political retreat.

Ethical imagination does not mean moral grandstanding. It means the capacity to picture second- and third-order effects before they appear on dashboards. It is the habit of asking who will touch the rule next. Translate the abstraction. A reflective architect reads a designation list and imagines a help-desk queue. She reads a banking advisory and imagines a risk committee on a Friday afternoon. She asks what behaviour this text will trigger.

The compass matters here. Without it, incentives pull toward excess. Fear of enforcement encourages over-compliance. Distance dulls responsibility. The compass reorients choice.

A credible limitation must be addressed. Ethical imagination risks subjectivity. Different architects will imagine different harms. Reconciling this requires discipline. Imagination must be tethered to evidence. Testimony, data, and feedback loops anchor it. This is not empathy as intuition. It is empathy as method.

The biographies earlier revealed another trait: courage of revision. Reflective architects treat initial designs as hypotheses. When evidence contradicts intent, they adjust. This runs against bureaucratic instinct. Institutions prefer consistency. Yet rigidity breeds failure. Learning demands visible change.

Observe how this plays out in practice. A sanctions drafter receives field reports showing delayed medical imports. She can interpret them as noise. Or she can reopen language. Name the fork: defensive closure versus adaptive revision. Explain it: the first protects authorship; the second protects outcomes. The consequence determines whether harm accumulates quietly or attenuates.

The compass appears again. It does not eliminate risk. It guides recalibration.

There is also a social dimension. Reflective architects cultivate networks across silos. They speak to compliance desks, aid agencies, and investigators. Not performatively. Practically. Earlier we met practitioners sharing informal guidelines before formal reform. This matters. Institutions change slowly. Norms change faster.

A further quality emerges: temporal awareness. Sanctions architects work under urgency. Crises compress time. Reflective architects build slack before crises hit. They pre-author humanitarian channels. They rehearse licensing surges. They know that delay is itself a decision.

Metrics matter here. A reflective architect does not ask only how many entities were designated. She asks how long licences took. She tracks false positives. She counts abandoned transactions. According to the World Bank (2020), transaction costs can rise by double digits under broad measures. Architects who monitor such figures can intervene early.

The limitation returns once more. No architect controls the whole system. Banks, allies, and adversaries adapt. Reconciling this requires modesty. The reflective architect knows her influence is partial. That knowledge sharpens rather than weakens resolve.

The image of the next architect crystallises. She sits inside institutions, not above them. She drafts text with a pencil, not a pen, ready to erase. She treats silence as data. She resists the comfort of maximalism. She understands that cruelty often emerges not from intent but from inattention.

The closing choice is not abstract. It is immediate and testable. When the next sanctions package is drafted, who signs off on its feedback plan? Who owns its humanitarian metrics? Who has authority to revise language without reopening politics? If the answer is no one, authorship remains incomplete.

The compass points still. Toward restraint where possible. Toward pressure where necessary. Toward architects who know that systems bend according to the hands that build them.

About the Author

Selma Aarvik writes about the quiet places where law, finance, and ethics collide. Her work follows the people who design sanctions, staff compliance desks, and try to keep humanitarian channels open when political tempers run hot. Rather than treating sanctions as abstract policy, she looks at the biographies behind the spreadsheets: the case officers, data sleuths, and back-office staff whose decisions decide whether money moves or stalls. Growing up in a port city where older relatives spoke about embargoes and shortages, she learnt early that trade rules were felt first in kitchens and chemists, not just in parliaments. Her writing brings that historical memory to bear on today's weaponised finance, asking who carries the moral weight when economic tools become instruments of pressure. Across her work, she aims to equip readers to see sanctions as human-made systems that can be redesigned, not as automatic responses to every crisis.

www.ingramcontent.com/pod-product-compliance
Lightning Source LLC
Chambersburg PA
CBHW031345230926
51848CB00002B/389
9789376558230